Fraud Markers, De-banking, and Financial Crime

This book enlightens the reader as to how the financial sector in the UK operates fraud databases to help combat fraud and explains the phenomenon of 'debanking'. It considers the unique confluence of necessity, a flexible regulatory framework, and recent history of collaboration that now places fraud databases and data-sharing at the heart of the UK's multi-agency counter-fraud strategy. It offers a practical slant to the theory behind the secretive counter-fraud and money-laundering investigation techniques, technology, and practices employed by financial organisations to disrupt fraud and money laundering. The work explains how and why the UK leads the world in this field, what progress is being made internationally to replicate these systems, and the legislative hurdles that need to be overcome to enable the level of data sharing required to make fraud databases operationally successful. It also explores the worrying trends and practices in the systems used which have adversely impacted on both innocent parties and the victims of fraud. Drawing on real-life examples, the book explores the benefits of transparency and whether the databases and the organisations that utilise them can better build fairness into their systems. It will be an invaluable resource for researchers, practitioners and policy-makers working in the areas of counter-fraud and anti-money laundering.

Jeremy Asher is a practising solicitor who has specialised in criminal and regulatory law for more than 25 years. Since 2020 he has developed a practice in challenging fraud markers that have been unfairly or erroneously loaded against individuals by banks and other financial organisations. He is also Founder and Chairman of the Financial Fraud Awareness Campaign and is a director of the community interest company that manages it.

The Law of Financial Crime

Series Editors:
Nicholas Ryder
Professor of Law, Cardiff University, School of Law and Politics, UK.

Dr. Lachmi Singh
Associate Lecturer, Bristol Law School, University of the West of England, UK.

Sam Bourton
Lecturer in Law, the University of the West of England, UK.

While a growing number of high profile financial crime cases have hit the headlines recently the topic of financial crime is also generating much attention amongst academics and practitioners. This series will be the first to be dedicated to the law of financial, or economic, crime and offers a platform for important and original research in this area.

Books in the series will cover traditional Subjects of financial crime including money laundering, terrorist financing, fraud, market abuse, insider dealing, market manipulation, tax evasion, bribery and corruption. But broader legal and regulatory issues will also be covered as well as emerging areas of concern such as the risks to stability of the financial system posed by financial crime. Emphasis will be placed on comparative approaches to the Subject considering legislation across a number of jurisdictions as well as international regulations where appropriate, giving the series a truly global outlook.

The titles in the series are primarily aimed at an audience of researchers, scholars and practitioners in the area but should also be of interest to policy makers, law enforcement agencies, financial regulatory agencies, as well as people employed within the financial services sector.

Available titles in this series include:

Competition Law and Financial Crime
A Comparative Analysis of International Responses to Market Manipulation
Diana Johnson

Fraud Markers, De-banking, and Financial Crime
A Legal Analysis of Counter-fraud Practices in the UK and Beyond
Jeremy Asher

For more information about this series, please visit: www.routledge.com/The-Law-of-Financial-Crime/book-series/FINCRIME

Fraud Markers, De-banking, and Financial Crime

A Legal Analysis of Counter-fraud Practices in the UK and Beyond

Jeremy Asher

Routledge
Taylor & Francis Group
LONDON AND NEW YORK

First published 2025
by Routledge
4 Park Square, Milton Park, Abingdon, Oxon OX14 4RN

and by Routledge
605 Third Avenue, New York, NY 10158

Routledge is an imprint of the Taylor & Francis Group, an informa business

British Library Cataloguing-in-Publication Data
A catalogue record for this book is available from the British Library

Library of Congress Cataloging-in-Publication Data
Names: Asher, Jeremy (Lawyer), author.
Title: Fraud markers, de-banking, and financial crime : a legal analysis of counter-fraud practices in the UK and beyond / Jeremy Asher.
Description: Abingdon, Oxon [UK] ; New York, NY : Routledge, 2025. | Series: The law of financial crime | Includes bibliographical references and index.
Identifiers: LCCN 2024057936 (print) | LCCN 2024057937 (ebook) | ISBN 9781032962054 (hardback) | ISBN 9781032962078 (paperback) | ISBN 9781003588542 (ebook)
Subjects: LCSH: Banking law—Great Britain—Criminal provisions. | Money Laundering—Law and legislation—Great Britain. | Fraud—Law and legislation—Great Britain.
Classification: LCC KD1737.R43 A89 2025 (print) | LCC KD1737.R43 (ebook) | DDC 345.41/0263–dc23/eng/20241205
LC record available at https://lccn.loc.gov/2024057936
LC ebook record available at https://lccn.loc.gov/2024057937

ISBN: 978-1-032-96205-4 (hbk)
ISBN: 978-1-032-96207-8 (pbk)
ISBN: 978-1-003-58854-2 (ebk)

DOI: 10.4324/9781003588542

Typeset in Times New Roman
by Apex CoVantage, LLC

I dedicate this book to my wife, Maria, who has stood by me through thick and thin for more than 30 years. She listened to my initial concerns about the injustice I saw being caused by fraud markers, and she inspired the schools' project (out of which was born the Financial Fraud Awareness Campaign), and provided practical solutions and encouragement at every step of the way.

Maria gave me the idea for this book and through discussion and editing has helped me to bring it into being.

Many weekends – and much of a Christmas – have been sacrificed along the way, and it has been a real team effort.

Thank you x

Contents

Foreword

Having been on the receiving end of a number of Cifas markers over the years (and, in my case, rightly so), I can attest to their ability to totally hamstring an offender. Within minutes of a marker being loaded by a financial institution, all of the Subject's bank accounts are either suspended or entirely closed. And in the vast majority of cases, the financial institutions will refuse to discuss with the Subject the reasons for their accounts being closed. The impact of having a marker loaded can endure for the best part of a decade.

In my experience, a Cifas marker imposes an even greater degree of restriction than a Freezing Injunction (of which I have also been on the receiving end). Readers might be aware that Lord Justice Donaldson described Freezing Injunctions as the law's 'nuclear weapons' (in *Bank Mellat v Nikpour [1985] FSR 87*).

I raise this point because, under the terms of a Freezing Injunction, the Subject can continue to withdraw funds for day-to-day living expenses and (in most cases) a reasonable sum for legal fees. Furthermore, Freezing Injunctions can only be granted upon application to a senior judge and on the basis that the applicant makes a cross-undertaking in damages (in case the injunction is obtained improperly).

But Cifas markers give no such flexibility and do not have to be made on application to a court. There is no requirement, at all, for any undertaking in damages.

It is clear, therefore, that where Cifas markers are loaded improperly or erroneously, this can cause the Subject a considerable degree of chaos, in circumstances where there is no apparent avenue of appeal. And that is why Jeremy Asher's work in this field is so important.

This enlightening book explores Cifas markers in detail and lifts the veil on the secretive realm in which they sit. It is hard to imagine something more devastating than a nuclear bomb but, if such a thing exists, it surely ought to be handled with a far greater level of care than the bomb itself.

This book is a 'must read' for anybody either studying or working in finance, banking, or commercial law – or, indeed, any person or organisation with a bank account!

Alexander WOOD
(Keynote Speaker, Writer and FinCrime Expert)
London

Acknowledgements

Many people have encouraged me to write this book, and I would like to thank everyone for their patience and belief in me. The list would go on for pages so I will keep my acknowledgments short.

Writing a book takes far more time than I ever imagined and without my wonderful wife, Maria's, support and encouragement, it would not have happened at all.

Richard Swarbrick deserves special mention for beer-infused perspective and enthusiasm towards 'Asher on Fraud', for his unswerving sense of public duty, and his vision that has helped to bring the Financial Fraud Awareness Campaign to life.

Enormous thanks to Alex Wood for his special insight which has proved extremely helpful and for his sense of humour and commitment to the cause.

Thanks go to Robert Brooker who introduced me to the contacts who have helped me develop the schools' project into what it has become, and for his belief in me and my book.

Thanks to my daughter, Freya and her partner, Hugh and our great friends Abigail and Richard Wells who have all provided stimulating academic debate and support.

Thanks also to my good buddy Douglas Morgan for his transatlantic encouragement and help with research.

Thanks to Professor Mark Button for contacting me out of the blue and Professor Ian Ross for his steadfast support on LinkedIn and willingness to assist.

It is an honour to have my work included in this prestigious academic series. Dr Sam Manfort suggested the book become an academic tome, provided me with guidance, and introduced me to Routledge. Professor Lachmi Singh suggested the format. Professor Nic Ryder saw its relevance within the series and has helped push it forward.

Finally but by no means least, thanks to Pim, our Golden Retriever, for helping to keep me sane in her own inimitable way!

Abbreviations (where repeated)

ADR	Alternative Dispute Resolution
AI	Artificial Intelligence
AML	Anti-Money Laundering
ABI	Association of British Insurers
APP	Authorised Push Payment Fraud
BBB	British Business Bank
BEIS	The department of Business, Energy and Industrial Strategy
BBLS	Bounce Back Loan Scheme
BBRS	Business Banking Resolution Service
CBML	Cash-Based Money Laundering
CBILS	Coronavirus Business Interruption Loan Scheme
CCFF	Covid Corporate Financing Facility
CCJ	County Court Judgment
CLBILS	Coronavirus Large Business Interruption Scheme
CPIA	Criminal Procedure and Investigations Act 1996
CPS	Crown Prosecution Service
ECCTA	Economic Crime and Corporate Transparency Act 2013
ECHR	European Convention of Human Rights
FATF	Financial Action Task Force
FBI	Federal Bureau of Investigations
FCA	Financial Conduct Authority
FELEG	Five Eyes Law Enforcement Group
FinCEN	The Financial Crimes Enforcement Network (US)
FMSA	Financial Services and Markets Act 2000
FOS	Financial Ombudsman Service
FPS	Faster Payment System
GDPR	General Data Protection Regulation
HBOS	Halifax Bank Of Scotland
HMRC	His Majesty's Revenue & Customs
ICO	Information Commissioner's Office
IFR	Insurance Fraud Register
IMTO	International Money Transfer Organisations

KYC	Know Your Customer
MLRO	Money Laundering Reporting Officer
NCA	National Crime Agency
NATIS	National Investigation Service
PACE	Police & Criminal Evidence Act 1984
PAYE	Pay As You Earn
PEP	Politically Exposed Person
PPI	Payment Protection Insurance
PSR	Payment Systems Regulator
SAR	Suspicious Activity Report
SEC	The Securities and Exchange Commission
SLAPP	Strategic Litigation Against Public Participation
SME	Small Medium Enterprises
SRA	Solicitors Regulation Authority
UKFIU	UK Financial Intelligence Unit

1 An introduction to the fraud databases

The aim of this book is to explain how the financial sector in the UK operates fraud databases to help combat fraud and, also, to explain the phenomenon of '*debanking*'. It considers the unique confluence of necessity, a flexible regulatory framework, and recent history of collaboration that now places fraud databases and data-sharing at the heart of the UK's multi-agency counter-fraud strategy. It offers a practical slant to the theory behind the counter-fraud and money laundering[1] investigation techniques, technology, law, and practices used by financial organisations to disrupt fraud and money laundering. The book explores how and why the UK leads the world in this field, what progress is being made internationally to replicate these systems, and the legislative hurdles that need to be overcome to enable the level of data sharing required to make fraud databases operationally successful. However, worrying trends and practices have emerged in the use of these systems which have adversely impacted on both innocent parties and the victims of fraud. In such cases the injustice and hardship caused can be devastating rather than deserved, as some selected real-life examples demonstrate. The book explores whether the databases and the organisations that utilise them can better build transparency and fairness into their systems. It is not intended to be a practical guide to assist those seeking to remove fraud markers.

The book answers the following questions:

- is it right for private organisations to have unfettered 'state powers' over civilians, which sometimes exceed Article 8 ECHR principles?[2]
- would greater transparency mean that many financial offences will be prevented from happening in the first place?
- is it right for the standard of proof for loading markers to be below that of criminal standard?

1 See Chapter 2 for detailed analysis of the practice of hiding criminal property.
2 See Chapter 5 for detailed discussion; Article 8 covers the rights to privacy and family life.

DOI: 10.4324/9781003588542-1

Background

The banking and finance industry is in the international spotlight because, as technology expands across the globe, so does the threat posed by organised crime. The UK was the first country to embrace a Faster Payments System (FPS),[3] which, while enabling quicker and more intuitive banking which is popular with customers, is equally popular with criminals. The threat and the astronomical losses suffered to criminals is enormous. In its comprehensive review of the fraud landscape, in November 2022 the House of Lords'[4] Fraud Act 2006 Digital Fraud Committee *Fighting Fraud: Breaking the Chain*[5] report ('Breaking the Chain Report') found that 41% of criminal offences were fraud related, and fraud costs the economy billions of pounds every year. The committee found that during the COVID-19 pandemic, fraud had increased by 25%.

In consequence, to help fight fraud and counter money laundering in the UK, fraud databases and data sharing capabilities have been developed and utilised by a multi-agency public-private partnership. The capability, systems and perceived success of these systems has come to the attention of countries around the world, some of whom have developed similar systems or have expressed a desire to do so.

Fraud markers are a simple enough concept. Once a financial organisation is alerted to a potential fraudulent transaction or application, they will immediately block that transaction or place the application on hold. They will then investigate, and then if they are satisfied that a financial crime is in progress or has been committed by the account holder or applicant, they will shut down the account in question or reject the application. They will then load the details of the account holder or applicant (known as the data Subject)[6] to a fraud database. The databases therefore provide warning systems to help organisations decide whether an applicant or customer is safe to provide services to, such as when an application for finance or banking services is made or where organisations conduct reviews of their customer databases. The databases have become the first line of defence in the fight against fraud and money

3 Faster Payments means real time payments that must arrive by the end of the next businessday–seewww.wearepay.uk/what-we-do/payment-systems/faster-payment-system/how-faster-payments

4 The House of Lords is the second chamber of UK Parliament; its members are unelected, chosen by present and past governments to question government actions and examine bills of parliament (bills are proposed laws which when passed into law become Acts of Parliament); see www.parliament.uk/business/lords/

5 www.publications.parliament.uk/pa/ld5803/ldselect/ldfraudact/87/8702.htm

6 Subject(s), or data Subject, is the term used throughout this book to denote the customer of an organisation or an applicant for banking or other financial products and services. Organisations hold data on account holders and applicants, and together they are considered by the Data Protection Act 2018 to be Subjects.

laundering since they prevent suspects from obtaining credit or banking facilities for up to six years and so disrupt criminal activity. Banks are under a duty to report those suspected of money laundering to the National Crime Agency (NCA).[7]

Most fraud markers are hidden from sight behind credit ratings. Subjects are not notified when markers have been loaded against them by banks, and some may be unaware of them for many years since they only come to light if accounts are closed or applications for finance are refused.

For those wishing to challenge markers that have been loaded against them, there is no equality of arms and no right to a fair trial.[8] The organisations that load markers – and the fraud databases they use – are generally secretive about what they do and how they operate. The organisations that develop and sell their databases to the finance industry will not publish their handbooks, let alone allow lawyers to have copies of them. There is a reverse burden of proof placed upon the Subject to prove their innocence and many Subjects discover they have lost the evidence that would have supported their appeals against the markers.

The closure of bank accounts and denial of credit facilities commonly results in people losing their jobs or businesses. Due to anti-human slavery legislation, employees now need their own bank accounts before they can be paid or commence employment. Those working in financial services who have had markers loaded against them face instant dismissal and are effectively blacklisted from employment in the sector. Such fraud markers can be used against those who have been dismissed for 'relevant conduct' that is frequently not fraud related at all. People who have been marked can lose their homes and families. Many of those marked suffer from poor mental health. Fraud markers therefore act as a restriction on a Subject's liberty. The increased use of fraud markers risks creating an economic subclass, with associated long-term adverse implications for our society.

Many organisations that load fraud markers do not conduct thorough investigations. The standard of proof they work to is based on a civil balance of probabilities test that allows for the use of assumptions. Genuinely innocent people can be caught in the fraud marker net. Throughout the book I will provide some examples and case studies from my practice where expedient and necessary to offer explanation, but out of respect for my clients' privacy, I have anonymised all their details. Few of the cases I am writing about have been 'reported' on the Financial Ombudsman Service's (FOS)[9] website. Many of my cases are resolved directly with the organisation that loaded the marker.

7 www.nationalcrimeagency.gov.uk

8 Article 6 European Convention of Human Rights; discussed in more detail in Chapter 5.

9 See www.financial-ombudsman.org.uk, an independent public body established by part XVI and schedule 17 of the Financial Services and Markets Act 2000 (as amended)

The cases – and the appeal mechanisms that must be followed – are anything but straightforward. Furthermore, my clients are frequently reluctant to speak openly about their experiences because, even though they may have had markers removed, they are concerned about the social stigma of having had a fraud marker loaded against them; only one of my clients has ever spoken to a journalist.

The injustice caused through financial organisations loading fraud markers against genuinely innocent Subjects is likely to be wider than that caused by the Post Office[10] Horizon scandal.[11] More than 700 Subpostmasters were wrongly prosecuted and convicted of fraud related offences following private prosecutions brought by the Post Office which failed to disclose failures in its computer systems.

In the UK the scale of the problem of people being debanked is vast. In 2022, the FCA confirmed that 343,000 accounts were closed in the UK,[12] and by the mid-point of 2023 nearly 200,000 more had been closed.

As I will explain later there is a difference between the use of fraud markers and the de-banking of high Politically Exposed Persons (PEPs) as complained about publicly by certain politicians.

How the systems operate

Financial institutions use many tools to help them to detect fraud and money laundering and to help fraud investigators to make decisions. Banks are probably right to be secretive about their intelligence gathering tools. What I do know is that, when they investigate, banks use a combination of algorithms, artificial intelligence (AI), fraud reports from other financial institutions and law enforcement agencies, and information contained in other fraud databases to assist them. Depending on the source of the funds or the nature of the transaction in question, banks also make assumptions. The technology is used to understand consumer behaviour and flag characteristics that might indicate higher risk, for example where several accounts are opened in a particular postcode location. They also monitor transactions, flagging when account limits might be reached or those which are considered 'abnormal' to the account in question. 'False positive alerts' for financial crimes such as fraud, theft, or money laundering are then investigated, during which time accounts are frozen before decisions are reached about whether to continue offering the Subject services.

10 The Post Office offers a range of postal, banking and payments services from branches across the UK. Subpostmasters are self-employed and take on a licence to run Post Office branches. See www.postoffice.co.uk

11 For background context of the scandal see www.bbc.co.uk/news/business-56718036.

12 See www.telegraph.co.uk/news/2023/07/31/nigel-farage-all-banks-guilty-debanking-fca-coutts-account/

The police in the UK now acknowledge that the scale of the fraud and money laundering problem is so vast that it is impossible to arrest its way out of the backlog. Several different tactics are used in both the public and private sectors to detect fraud and then disrupt it. Fraud markers are the front-line first response disruptive measure in that fight against fraud. What better way than to close suspicious bank accounts and make it difficult for the controllers of those accounts to operate financially for up to six years?

Take this simplistic example: a student bank account has £20,000 suddenly arrive in it. The bank quickly investigates the source of those funds to identify whether it was likely to be a genuine transaction or not. It seems unusual because it is a lot of money going into a student account, and the transaction will have been picked up quickly by data analysis programmes. If the bank had reasonable suspicion to consider that the funds were from a fraudulent source, it would block the transaction, close the account, and then load the details of the Subject to databases which can be analysed by other financial organisations to help them when making decisions about whether to offer finance or accounts. Depending on the circumstances it will also submit a Suspicious Activity Report (SAR) to the NCA. In this scenario it is highly unlikely to contact the Subject who will only realise something is wrong when they cannot access their account.

Unless the Subject is identified as a victim of fraud, the loading of these details into the fraud databases is kept hidden from view on credit reports. The Subject is not told about the loading and may only find out about them when they apply for credit and banking facilities at some date in the future or if their other bank accounts are closed.

Professor Mark Button, Dr David Shepherd and Dean Blackbourn described fraud markers as 'a form of "grey" justice and punishment' in their work: *The Fraud 'Justice Systems': A Scoping Study on the Civil, Regulatory and Private Paths to 'Justice' for Fraudsters; Main Report November 2016.*[13] They argued that such markers 'criminalise' Subjects in the eyes of organisations to which they apply for finance and credit. They are akin to the type of fixed penalty notices that are imposed in the criminal justice system, such as by the police in relation to minor motoring offences. However, there are important distinctions, not least that fraud markers are issued without notice, they are secretive, and there is no right to judicial oversight at the time a marker is loaded. Contrast the driver of a vehicle suspected of speeding; they are allowed to challenge the evidence at the outset, accept the proposed penalty, seek an alternative penalty (such as a speed awareness course), or ask a court to decide whether the penalty was lawful. The punishment aspect of fraud markers is through the Subject being barred from obtaining mainstream

13 www.pure.port.ac.uk/ws/portalfiles/portal/5069284/Fraud_Justice_Systems_2016_Final_Report_1_.pdf

credit and banking facilities or by having to pay a premium should they be lucky enough to find an organisation willing to accept the higher risk posed.

Ostensibly the three searchable organisations that provide such database or warning flag tools to the finance industry are: Cifas, National Hunter, and Synectics Solutions SIRA. There are many organisations that provide intelligence services to banks that are not searchable. Professor Button's report helpfully provides a non-exhaustive list of the fraud detection databases he was able to identify which are as follows: Cifas; Claims and Underwriting Exchange (which is now linked to the Motor Insurers Bureau);[14] College of Policing Disapproved Register; Dun and Bradstreet Critical Intelligence Solution; Elixir 2000;[15] Equifax Fraud Protector (known as Shield); Experian National Fraud Database;[16] Facewatch; Fraud Intelligence Network (FIN); Health Insurers Fraud Investigation Database; Insurance Fraud Network; Insurance Fraud Investigators Group; Insurance Fraud Register (IFR);[17] Lawyers Against Fraud; National Anti-Fraud Network; National Business Crime Solution; National Fraud Initiative (via Synectics Solutions); National Fraud Intelligence Bureau (hosted by City of London Police); National SIRA (via Synectics Solutions); Netfoil; Telecommunication United Kingdom Fraud Forum; and Thomson Reuters World Check. In addition, Scamalytics[18] provides data on identifying romance scammers and IP addresses used in frauds, and Mastercard Consumer Fraud Risk[19] identifies in real time suspicious transactions, as does Unit 21.[20] However, there are likely to be other even more secretive databases that have yet to be identified.

The growth and development of these organisations can be traced back to Section 7A of Schedule 3 of The Data Protection Act 1988 which stated that the processing of sensitive data was lawful where it is 'necessary for the purposes of preventing fraud' when conducted as 'a member of an anti-fraud organisation'. That legislation has been superseded and developed over the years, notably through General Data Protection Regulation (GDPR)[21] and the Data Protection Act 2018[22] which enabled GDPR in the UK.[23] The processing of personal data is considered a legitimate interest in fraud detection.

14 Searchable through the MIB www.mib.org.uk/managing-insurance-data/mib-managed-services/cue-miaftr
15 Searchable www.crifdecisionsolutions.co.uk/products-and-services/elixir-intelligence/
16 Searchable wwe.experian.co.uk/privacy/privacy-policies?utm_medium=internalRef&utm_source=Consumer%20Services
17 Searchable www.theifr,org.uk/en/faqs/#2139
18 Searchable www.scamalytics.com
19 www.mastercardservices.com/en/industries/financial-institutions/insights/fight-fraud-real-time-product-level-data
20 www.unit21.ai/solutions/fraud-detection
21 GDPR is an international concept, as discussed later in this book
22 www.legislation.gov.uk/ukpga/2018/12/contents/enacted
23 For commentary see www.ico.org.uk

Anyone applying for financial services, insurance or even a job will be familiar with clauses known as 'fair processing notices' in the application process confirming that their data will be shared.

The reason Subjects are not informed when they have been marked is due to organisations believing that they could commit offences of 'tipping off'.[24]

Cifas

Cifas[25] (pronounced with the *I* rather than C*ee*fas) operates the largest and most transparent database. Cifas was set up in 1988, when it was known as the *Credit Industry Fraud Avoidance Scheme*. It is a not-for-profit organisation; its last accounts revealed a turnover of £10 million. By 2021 it was recording more than £1 billion worth of fraudulent transactions a year.

Cifas is authorised as an anti-fraud organisation under Section 40(3)(a) of the Immigration Act 2014. An anti-fraud organisation is defined by section 6(8) of the Serious Crime Act 2007 as 'an organisation which enables or facilitates any sharing of information to prevent fraud or a particular kind of fraud or which has any of these functions as its purpose or one of its purposes'. Its function is defined as to maintain a database of disqualified persons from information supplied to it by the Secretary of State. Banks and building societies use this database for status checks against disqualified persons; they may not provide such disqualified persons with financial services or accounts. Cifas has a duty to provide the Financial Conduct Authority (FCA)[26] with quarterly reports.

Cifas is a Member of the Joint Fraud Task Management Board, an organisation that is chaired by the Home Office and which includes the British Bankers Association, City of London Police, Financial Fraud Action UK, the NCA (Britain's version of the FBI)[27] and Victim Support,[28] plus banks. According to its website, Cifas 'aims to protect the public and businesses from financial fraud, reduce the effects of fraud on victims and increase the prosecution of fraudsters'.

It also operates the Organised Fraud Intelligence Group[29] which enables the sharing of information among government, law enforcement, the financial sector, and other interested parties.

To give you some idea of scale, there are probably about two million Cifas markers in existence at any one time, with Cifas reporting in 2022 that one

24 Section 333(1) Proceeds of Crime Act 2002
25 www.cifas.org.uk
26 See www.fca.org.uk
27 See www.fbi.gov
28 www.victimsupport.org.uk
29 See www.cifas.org.uk/fraud-prevention-community/member-benefits/intelligence/ofig

marker was loaded nearly every 90 seconds. We know this because Cifas produces annual reports, and the statistics are always eye opening: in 2016 it recorded 325,000 cases of fraud; in 2017 it recorded 305,000; in 2018 there were 324,000; in 2019 there were 364,000; then 310,000 in 2020; another 360,000 in 2021; rising to 409,000 in 2022;[30] and falling to 374,100 in 2023.[31] Most markers last for six years.[32]

Cifas operates two databases:

The National Fraud Database has more than one thousand members,[33] including all the High Street banks,[34] the Home Office,[35] recruitment consultancies, letting agents, insurers, some accountancy firms, and other suppliers of financial services. Members record suspected incidents of fraud and money laundering to the database. Some organisations that are not themselves members will engage organisations that are members to conduct due diligence services for them. Frequently member organisations will dismiss employees instantly when they discover they have Cifas markers recorded against them; I have seen numerous accountants and those working in finance face this predicament.

Until about November 2022 cases filed to the National Fraud Database[36] had to be supported by evidence and meet the 'four pillars' of Principle 4 of the Standard of Proof.[37] The Standard of Proof that applied was:

1. that there are reasonable grounds to believe that a fraud or financial crime has been committed or attempted
2. that the evidence must be clear, relevant and rigorous such that the member could confidently report the conduct of the Subject to the police
3. the conduct of the Subject must meet the criteria of one of the case types
4. in order to file the member must have rejected, withdrawn, or terminated a product on the basis of fraud unless the member has an obligation to provide the product or the Subject has already received the full benefit of the product

30 See data published generally and www.fraudscape.co.uk/?utm_campaign=CifasPressReleaseFs23
31 See 661e5650fdbfbcc31e8ab3c6_Cifas Fraudscape 2024 Downloadable Report.pdf (website-files.com)
32 See further discussion in Chapter 5 – some markers are now loaded for shorter periods of time
33 See list www.cifas.org.uk/services/national-fraud-database/national-fraud-database-members
34 There are very few banks that are not members of Cifas; non-members tend to be new organisations such as payment service providers which are not yet recognised as banks, but over time all tend to join Cifas, the latest examples being Pockit and Revolut (which is not yet a bank)
35 The Government department responsible for national security and economic stability www.gov.uk/government/organisations/home-office
36 The title Cifas gives to its database
37 See www.cifas.org.uk/fraud-prevention-community/member-benefits/data/nfd/nfd-principles

The Standard of Proof that applies now is:

1. that there are reasonable grounds to believe that a fraud or financial crime has been committed or attempted
2. that the evidence must be clear, relevant, and rigorous
3. the conduct of the Subject must meet the criteria of one of the case types
4. in order to file the member must have rejected, withdrawn, or terminated a product on the basis of fraud unless the member has an obligation to provide the product or the Subject has already received the full benefit of the product

The question of whether it was right and fair for Cifas to amend this standard of proof is a recurring theme in this book. Clearly there has been a reduction from a criminal standard of proof to a civil standard. I believe Cifas amended the burden of proof for three reasons: first, it is a commercial organisation that is in competition with other providers, notably Synectics Solutions and National Hunter. Second, Cifas has had to pander to its members who now use AI and automated processes, which themselves are under increased financial pressure; the use of automated investigative tools is far less expensive for the smaller, challenger banks than operating a large, highly trained and skilled workforce to conduct investigations to a criminal standard. Third, some of its members were confused by the standard of proof, as was obvious when I was working on cases before the changes came in. The standard of proof expected investigations to have been conducted to a standard which the police would recognise, and frankly it became apparent that that was beyond the capabilities of many members of Cifas.

Why should Cifas' members not work to the same higher standards as the police? After all, when loading markers Cifas' members are accusing data Subjects of criminal conduct, and as 577,000 Suspicious Activity Reports to the National Crime Agency demonstrate, they do report cases to the police. Therefore, shouldn't they justify such decisions to the criminal standard? Was that decision made by Cifas to reduce the standard unethical and wrong?

The case types identified by Cifas are as follows:

1. *Protective registration*. This is a marker that you can pay for directly to Cifas or a third-party provider, if you believe you have been a victim of fraud. It lasts for two years
2. *Victim of impersonation*. This is a marker filed by a lender for your protection if you have been a victim of identity fraud. It lasts for 13 months
3. *First-party fraud*. This can be filed when there is no intent to repay promised future repayment for exchanging goods and/or services. It can last up to six years
4. *Facility takeover*. This marker is filed when a bank account is taken over and used for unauthorised transactions, lasting for up to six years

5. *Misuse of facility*. This occurs when an account is obtained with the intent to use it for fraud or where it is used for a fraudulent purpose. It lasts for up to six years
6. *Asset conversion*. This marker can be filed when an individual sells goods that they do not own, for example, a car, under a hire purchase, conditional sale, contract hire, or leasing or rental agreement. It can last for up to six years
7. *Application fraud*. This marker can be filed when an application for credit is made using an individual's real name but false details such as employment, salary, address, or falsified documents. It can last for up to six years
8. *Insurance claims fraud*. When incorrect information is provided when seeking a monetary insurance claim, this marker may be filed, lasting for up to six years

The *Internal Threat Database*[38] is used by organisations in the finance sector and public sector to mark what are believed to be fraudulent employees, either because they have made fraudulent applications for positions or because they have acted fraudulently whilst at work. Those dismissed for gross misconduct can also be marked. The idea is to root out internal threats. Cifas reported that in 2023 there were 325 individuals recorded to the Insider Threat Database.

The standard of proof for loading markers to the internal database is different to that of the external fraud database: cases filed to the Internal Fraud Database must be supported by evidence and meet the 'four pillars' of Principle 4 of the Standard of Proof, and all four of the following conditions need to be met:

1. there are reasonable grounds to believe that a fraud or relevant conduct has been committed or attempted
2. the evidence must be clear, relevant and rigorous such that the member could confidently report the conduct of the Subject to the police or a relevant regulatory body or considers the fraud or relevant conduct as gross misconduct
3. the conduct of the Subject must meet the criteria of one of the case types
4. to file a case, the member must have

    a. declined employment; or
    b. withdrawn employment; or
    c. identified a fraud or relevant conduct after staff have left employment

The case types for the internal fraud database are as follows:

1. account fraud
2. being bribed

38 See www.cifas.org.uk/services/insider-threat-database/insider-threat-database-members

3. dishonest action by staff to obtain a benefit by theft or deception
4. employment application fraud (unsuccessful)
5. employment application fraud (successful)
6. unlawful obtaining or disclosure of commercial data
7. unlawful obtaining or disclosure of personal data

All such internal fraud database markers last for six years and may prevent the Subjects from obtaining some financial services, but this is case and application dependent.

Cifas offers an arbitration system, although it is impossible to discuss cases with its investigators because they are hidden from direct communication by a front-facing contact centre.[39] However, Cifas' arbitration system is limited in scope to deciding whether the organisation in question correctly followed procedure.

One of my clients, who was innocent of wrongdoing and who managed to persuade Cifas to overrule a marker that an organisation had refused to remove voluntarily, was so concerned that they made a Freedom of Information Act request to Cifas to ascertain whether they were part of a wider miscarriage of justice. Their Member of Parliament, Rebecca Long-Bailey, elicited a response from Cifas that confirmed that, in 2022, 868 requests were made to it to review a marker, of which 144 were removed. That equates to 16.6%. Cifas was not able to break down its figures to the number of individual Subjects loaded with markers.[40]

Challenges must be commenced against the organisations that load the markers before appeals to Cifas and FOS can be considered. I have not seen any figures published revealing the number of markers that are removed voluntarily by its members, but there will be substantially more cases fitting that category than Cifas has reported.

Synectics Solutions

Synectics Solutions[41] was established in 1992; it claims to have prevented £5 billion worth of fraud in the past 30 years and states that it works with more than 160 tier one banks, insurance companies, FTSE 250 companies, and the Cabinet Office.[42] In 2021 it posted a turnover of £22.97 million, its income

39 Practical attempts to discuss cases direct with Cifas have always failed.

40 Cifas' response to the FOIA request by Rebecca Long-Bailey MP is protected by client confidentiality.

41 See www.synectics-solutions.com/

42 See www.gov.uk/government/organisations/cabinet-office – a government ministerial department that supports the Prime Minister and ensures the effective running of government and is the corporate headquarters for government, in partnership with HM Treasury

being higher than Cifas because it also conducts on-boarding functions,[43] KYC,[44] and AML[45] services to its clients.

It runs two systems. The first is *National SIRA*, which is described on its website as 'the largest syndicated database of cross sector customer risk intelligence in the UK', with more than 160 members. The second system is the management of the data syndication program (sic) for the Cabinet Office under the National Fraud Initiative which collates data from public sector organisations, such as benefit claimants and Blue Badge holders.

In both instances, Synectics Solutions processes personal data collected by member organisations to verify identity. It uses automated machine-learning tools to: decide whether behaviour is consistent with that of known fraudsters; consider whether information submitted by the Subject is inconsistent with previous applications they have made; or consider if a persons' true identity has been hidden. In other words, it allows the use of assumptions without any other evidence required to support the loading. This tool allows for certain types of applications, in particular vehicle financing, as well as decisions regarding affordability and whether it is likely that the terms of loan agreement will be abided by, to be considered using automated decision-making processes. Organisations using these tools use logic, algorithms, and data from credit reference agencies to consider likely behaviour against credit histories and compare data against others in similar circumstances. For example, if an application is received from a person working in a particularly niche area, then decisions may be rejected if the organisations do not have sufficient data about others in similar circumstances to confidently assess risk. Data Subjects have the right to request human intervention to review refused applications.

Like Cifas, Synectics Solutions is designated as a specified anti-fraud organisation by The Serious Crime Act 2007.

Synectics Solutions' markers are either *clear* or *refer* and show against applications made for finance or insurance. A clear marker lasts for three years and should not cause problems, but a refer marker lasts for six years and can cause serious problems. As with Cifas it is the members themselves who decide whether markers should be loaded or not; although you can apply to Synectics Solutions for the erasure of data, it will refer to the organisation that loaded the data unless it is apparent that the time limits for retention have been exceeded.

Synectics Solutions methodology is to operate a system signalling fraud risk in real time rather than operating a system of managing a database with deeper tools. Its markers have been used when organisations have seen other markers loaded on other databases, a practice I refer to as 'cross referring'.

43 The process of establishing a contractual relationship with the customer, agreement of terms and conditions, identification processing.

44 Know Your Customer – the practice of formally identifying and understanding the practices of a customer

45 Anti-Money Laundering – see later for wider explanation and discussion

National Hunter

National Hunter[46] was established in 1993 and is another 'not-for-profit' organisation. It does not operate a database as such but rather a scheme where myriad of its member organisations share information which can be used to conduct investigations. Its core business sectors are mortgages, current accounts, credit cards, unsecured loans, Motor and Asset Finance, Commercial Finance, Merchant Services, and savings. It does not publish a list of its members, but its membership is restricted to those who are full members of one of the following trade associations: UK Finance; Building Societies . . . Association; Finance and Leasing Association; Association of Short-Term Lenders; Association of British Insurers (ABI); and 36H (Peer-2Peer Lenders).

National Hunter's markers are *clear, refer, inconsistency*, and *suspicious*. *Refer* most likely denotes that there is evidence of a constituent part of fraud as defined by the Fraud Act. *Inconsistency* is loaded where information has not been supplied by an applicant to a financial product. It therefore acts as a checking mechanism and provides leads for members to investigate further. Products should not be declined just because a refer status has been loaded; members should make their own checks and decisions accordingly. This rule applies to Cifas too. In practice, however, banks and finance companies are risk averse and when they see such markers many will automatically decline applications or close accounts.

Unlike Synectic Solutions and Cifas, National Hunter is not a specified anti-fraud organisation with authority granted by the Serious Crime Act 2007. I cannot see where its power to share data is derived from, although it may be authorised as a 'data matching' organisation under Schedule 9 to the Local Audit and Accountability Act 2014.[47] It is likely that Cifas and Synectics Solutions are authorised under this legislation too.

Unlike Synectics Solutions, National Hunter has little presence on social media (its LinkedIn account currently lists about 40 followers, one of which is me). Like Synectics Solutions and Cifas it does not publish its Operators Guide. Like Synectics Solutions it does not offer an arbitration system.

Insurance Fraud Register

Members of the Insurance Fraud Register[48] record markers to a register like that operated by Cifas, thereby disrupting insurance fraudsters. It is available to more than 300 members of the Association of British Insurers, which operates the system; its membership accounts for 80% of the insurance

46 See www.nhunter.co.uk
47 www.legislation.gov.uk/ukpga/2014/2/contents/enacted
48 www.theifr.org.uk eifr.org.uk

market. Reports are made to the Insurance Fraud Bureau[49] which is another not-for-profit organisation. The IFR does not publish its rules but does publish the criteria used for loading the details of Subjects to the register. Details are held for five rather than six years, and again it is for the organisation that loaded the marker to consider whether it can be removed. Unlike banks, its members notify Subjects if their details have been recorded on the register. If applicants appear on the register, members may choose not to provide products, stating 'each member is at liberty to adopt its own approach'. Data from the register is shared and typically may be picked up by other lenders providing products such as mortgages and loans. As with the other databases, appeals against markers are lodged initially with the organisation that loaded the marker. Like Cifas, the IFR provides an arbitration system with onwards appeals considered by the FOS.

The test used by members of the IFR to load markers is as follows:

> Any party seeking to obtain a benefit under the terms of any insurance related product, service or activity can be shown, on a balance of probabilities, through its actions, to have made or attempted to make a gain or induced or attempted to induce a loss by intentionally and dishonestly:
>
> - making a false representation, and/or
> - failing to disclose information, and/or
> - having abused the relevant party. . .'s position
>
> And, one or more of the following outcomes has taken place which relates to the fraudulent act:
>
> - an insurance policy application has been refused
> - an insurance policy or contract has been voided, terminated or cancelled
> - a claim under an insurance policy has been repudiated
> - a successful prosecution for fraud, the tort of deceit or contempt of court has been brought
> - the relevant party has formally accepted his/her guilt in relation to the fraudulent act in question including, but not limited to, accepting a police caution
> - an insurer has terminated a contract or a non-contracted relationship/recognition with a supplier or provider
> - an insurer has attempted to stop/recover or refused a payment(s) made in relation to a transaction
> - an insurer has challenged or demonstrated that a change to standing policy data was made without the relevant customer. . .'s authority

49 www.insurancefraudbureau.org

Provided that:

> the relevant party has been notified that its claim has been repudiated, or relevant policy or contract voided, terminated, or cancelled, for reasons of fraud and/or it is in breach of the relevant terms and conditions relating to fraud within the relevant policy or contract.

The IFR operates a service for the victims of identity theft and refers Subjects to Cifas to apply for protective registration.

Cifas, Synectics Solutions, the IFR, and National Hunter are not governed by a regulatory body such as the FCA.

Equifax,[50] Transunion,[51] and Experian[52]

These are grouped together because they provide information to their members to assist them with identifying Subjects who may be involved in fraud or money laundering. They all provide credit scores.

Equifax Fraud Protector[53] verifies bank accounts and identity for the finance industry. It uses Synectics Solutions' National SIRA and others to scan databases providing its business members with information and alerts which they can then use to consider whether to approve or decline applications. Businesses can be Subjected to red alerts. Equifax is available to banks and financial services. Its primary use appears to be as to ascertain whether Subjects have 'been associated with fraudulent applications'. The markers are 'accept', 'fraudulent', 'suspect', and 'inconsistent'. The system also verifies whether ID and bank account details are correct.

The suite of information provided includes details of County Court[54] Judgments (CCJs),[55] insolvencies, and checking against the fraud databases. TransUnion checks against Cifas.

In Experian's case it provides fraud risk scores – utilising the National Hunter database – and fraud detection tools, such as FraudNet which identifies and assesses devices used in applications to highlight fraudulent activity.

A subsidiary of TransUnion, *iovation, Inc*[56] collates geolocation information to ascertain the location of IT devices and behavioural information regarding interaction with websites or mobile apps.

50 www.equifax.co.uk
51 www.transunion.co.uk
52 www.experian.co.uk
53 www.equifax.co.uk/business/equifax-fraud-protector/en_gb/
54 The County Court is the first tier of civil courts in England, Wales, and Northern Ireland
55 A County Court Judgment is made if debts are unpaid
56 newsroom.transunion.com/transunion-completes-acquisition-of-iovation/

Lexis Nexis

One of the databases used frequently by insurance companies, brokers, and other insurance intermediaries is Lexis Nexis.[57] It has several products. Threat Matrix assists with the authentication of the users of online services. It compares a wide range of data, including email addresses, phone numbers, ID, passwords, driving licence information, log-in activity, and transaction histories.

According to its website it also provides a service called *BehavioSec* which includes data on 'mouse movements, touch screen inputs, keystroke and key pressed data' which help to identify whether the user is a real human.

Another service it provides is *World Compliance and Accuity* which collates open-source[58] data to validate information it holds elsewhere. This can include details regarding insolvencies, court records, government watch lists, electoral registers and information regarding the ownership of businesses, employment histories, sanctions lists, public media, PEP information including flagging whether a Subject may be related to a PEP, and professional affiliations. Such information is useful for AML and compliance screening for financial services and payment service providers, and any other business where there is a need, such a law firms and accountancy practices. It is, as the name suggests, a tool that is available worldwide.

GB Group PLC

Another British based fraud database that can be used internationally is provided by GBG Group PLC[59] which provides data services to more than 50 countries. Among several products it provides a mobile phone to customer match service which is useful in preventing identity fraud. It also identifies suspicious email addresses and identifies mixed and manufactured digital identities. It apparently pools its data from 50 million or more data records from 'millions of global customer interactions'.

Appeal processes

The process of appealing a fraud marker is complicated.[60] It is the member organisations that load the markers, not the databases. To challenge such markers, Cifas recommends that Subjects contact the organisation that loaded the marker first to see what it has to say about it. However, I have seen huge

57 risk.lexisnexis.co.uk
58 Freely available such as online and public records
59 www.gbgplc.com
60 Description of the appeal processes is based on professional experience challenging markers.

numbers of Subjects write to organisations and simply ask for a marker to be removed or for a review of the decision to load the marker, without having the faintest idea of why a marker was loaded in the first place. I have also come across many people who have failed to put forward any evidence of their innocence or provide logical arguments for the organisations to consider. I have seen many Subjects refer to evidence they have but not produce it, and I have frequently seen organisations not ask to see that evidence before refusing to remove the markers. Occasionally Subjects get lucky when they ask for the organisation to review the marker, but asking for a review is not without significant risk, and in my experience many more fall at that first hurdle than succeed. Cases can be extremely complicated requiring full legal analysis and argument to succeed. Some organisations will load markers to all three databases, making the process even more complex.

Once an organisation makes a negative decision, which is that the marker was correctly loaded, it will issue a Final Response. It will state where the Subject may appeal, generally either Cifas (if the marker relates to Cifas), the FOS, or both. If the appeal route is through the FOS, the Subject has six months from the date of that letter to appeal. I have seen numerous Subjects attempt to appeal out of time and have their applications for appeal refused.

Cifas provides a mechanism whereby it will review decisions. It is not a formal arbitration system, since Cifas cannot be called independent, impartial or neutral given that it is the joint controller of the Subject's data. Even though it is not a formal arbiter, in practice member organisations and the Courts will attach significant weight to its decisions.

The Financial Ombudsman Service is the largest Ombudsman in the world. It was established by Parliament under by Part XVI of the Financial Services and Markets Act 2000 (FMSA). Section 225(1) of FMSA allows for a scheme to resolve complaints between consumers and financial businesses 'quickly with minimal formality by an independent person'. Section 228(2) states that complaints are to be determined to what is 'in the opinion of the Ombudsman' fair and reasonable in all the circumstances of the case. Section 229(2)(a) allows for compensation against respondents 'of such an amount as the Ombudsman considers fair compensation for loss or damage' suffered by the complainant and Section 230(4) leaves costs to 'the opinion of the Ombudsman'. In financial year 2021/2022 it received 165,263 complaints and had an income of £221.7 million.[61] It offers a free service to those wishing to bring complaints and can order compensation of up to £375,000, although in practice awards are negligible, if anything, when fraud markers are considered incorrectly loaded.

61 Figures taken from Financial Ombudsman Service Annual Report and Accounts for year ended 31 March 2022

The rules governing the FOS are complicated and are tied in with FCA rules. Sometimes this causes issues about whether the FOS has the power to consider a particular complaint. The relevant rule is known as Dispute Resolution Scheme (DISP)[62] which defines what an eligible complainant is: a consumer, a micro enterprise, charity, or guarantor. Rule DISP 2.7.6 is particularly important because it sets out 17 scenarios when an eligible complainant can access the FOS's services. I will not reproduce that list in full here because much of it is not relevant to fraud markers, and thankfully the FOS's online complaints procedure asks questions to identify when a complaint is eligible to be considered by it.

Rule DISP 2.7.6 is particularly important for company directors and sole trader business owners, for two reasons:

First, fraud markers are mostly loaded personally against the controlling minds of a business rather than the businesses themselves.[63] As a matter of law, individuals can form *Mens Rea*,[64] a guilty mind, whereas a company, while it is itself a legal entity, does not have the mental capacity to make decisions itself. Fraud is an offence which requires specific intent and dishonesty before it can be made out. For example, the citation in a Section 2 Fraud Act 2006 charge may read as follows: 'You, ABC, on X date, dishonestly made a false representation to Y, namely Z etc. . . . intending to make a gain for yourself or another'.

Second, the account is likely to be in the name of the business or company, in which case the business or company is the customer, not its director or owner.

Company directors or sole trader business owners who have found a marker loaded against them personally when their business account has been closed cannot take appeals to the FOS. I am concerned about this because the issues relating to fraud markers in such cases are not much different to those affecting individual consumers.

Appeals to the FOS are considered in a two-stage process. First, an investigator will form a provisional view. If that is not accepted by either party, which is the Subject bringing the appeal or the financial organisation, then the final decision will rest with an Ombudsman. That final decision is binding on both parties and is reported, anonymised, on the FOS' website. That website provides an intuitive search engine for results.[65] For example it reported 211

62 See www.handbook.fca.org.uk/handbook/DISP/2/7.html

63 There are occasional exceptions to this rule such as when strict liability offences rather than those requiring specific intent are alleged. Strict liability offences do not require mens rea – or intention. Examples include driving offences or many regulatory offences.

64 Required to form the necessary criminal intent to commit an offence

65 See www.financial-ombudsman.org.uk/decisions-case-studies/ombudsman-decisions/search?Keyword=Cifas&DateFrom=2023-06-01&DateTo=2024-06-01&IsUpheld%5B1%5D=1&Sort=relevance

final decisions for complaints relating to Cifas between 1 June 2023 and 1 June 2024, of which 63 were upheld. During the same period seven complaints related to National Hunter, of which four were upheld, and there were 279 complaints considered relating to the Insurance Fraud Register, of which 108 were upheld. No complaints were considered in relation to Synectic Solutions.

The only route to dispute an Ombudsman's final decision is through Judicial Review. This is a process whereby the appellant (the person bringing the appeal) asks the High Court to consider whether the appeal process was fair. That was confirmed in *R (on the application of Assurant General Insurance Ltd) v Financial Ombudsman Service Ltd and Others* [2023][66] when Singh LJ stated 'generally speaking, questions of fact are primarily for the Ombudsman to determine, Subject only to judicial review on conventional public law grounds such as irrationality or procedural unfairness'. Judicial Review is not an appeal; 'it does not therefore provide an opportunity simply to re-argue a case in front of the High Court'. That confirmed the established law set out in *R (Aviva Life & Pensions (UK) Ltd) v FOS [2017]*[67] that the Ombudsman must consider what is fair and reasonable in all the circumstances of the case, and if they wish to depart from the rules, regulations, guidance and codes of practice, they may do so provided they give clear reasoning for the decision. The Courts have therefore not sought to interfere with the parameters that FOS works within, which are set out in statute.

In the criminal justice system, where there is a hierarchy of courts, the most serious appeals are heard by the Court of Appeal or the Supreme Court which report decisions in legal journals.[68] Cases that are considered by an Ombudsman where a final decision has been reached are reported on the FOS' website. Those decisions are anonymised and are shorter and more simplistic than the unwieldy judgments issued by the appeal courts.

Alternatively, if you do not want an Ombudsman to make the final decision, you can take the case to court. Whereas the FOS and Cifas offer a free service, appealing through the courts is an expensive option. This is especially the case because the courts can make adverse costs orders against the person bringing the appeal if they have not followed available arbitration routes through Cifas, the IFR, the FOS or The Business Banking Resolution Service (BBRS)[69] and can stay proceedings[70] until alternative dispute resolution (ADR)

66 *R (on the application of Assurant General Insurance Ltd) v Financial Ombudsman Service and Others* [2023] EWCA Civ 1049

67 *R (on the application of Aviva Life & Pensions (UK) Limited v Financial Ombudsman Service and Others* [2017] EWHC 352 (Admin)

68 For example the All England Law Reports or Criminal Law Reports.

69 See www.thebbrs.org which may provide a route for arbitration for larger businesses, but it depends on the circumstances and whether the organisation that loaded the marker is a member of it. The scheme is due to close on 13 December 2024

70 'Stay proceedings' means to bring a court case to a temporary halt or suspend it altogether

procedures such as arbitration are concluded, provided that those ADR processes are proportionate and preserve the right to a judicial hearing.[71]

Obviously if those alternative routes are not available then adverse penalties do not apply but appeals through the courts are nevertheless expensive and not without risk. This is because after a letter before action is issued, it is likely that the organisation that loaded the marker will engage expensive lawyers, and if the Subject has not asked for a final decision by an Ombudsman or Cifas, the organisations will be strengthened in their resolve by a favourable initial decision from FOS or a negative decision from Cifas and will disclose that reasoning to the court. This places the Subject at significant risk that the court will order them to pay the organisation's (likely) substantial legal fees. Furthermore, if the court decides against the Subject, then it amounts to a CCJ and if the costs are not paid as ordered then that CCJ can remain on credits records for six years from judgment,[72] thereby extending the period during which the Subject will have difficulty accessing financial products and services. By contrast if an appeal is rejected by Cifas or FOS then no costs awards are made[73] and the marker will come to an end when its life cycle naturally expires.

The FOS is often far better placed to decide whether markers should be removed than the courts because few judges have experience of dealing with them, whereas the investigators and Ombudsmen are well versed in applying the rules and see large numbers of cases which helps them to quickly disseminate information and consider the issues. When cases can be presented in a well-argued manner, the FOS is more likely than the courts to reach a fair decision because the parameters of its remit are wider. However, as with the courts, unless cases are presented clearly and logically, Subjects are unlikely to obtain justice; I have read many FOS decisions where it is apparent that had the Subject had legal representation and presented their cases correctly then it is more likely that the FOS would have upheld their appeals. Issues also arise when the FOS is asked to consider compensation and costs. I have only had one case where the FOS ordered legal costs to be paid by a financial organisation. Its ability to decide on compensation is limited because of the amount of work its staff undertake, making this aspect of a case a lesser priority; I have known many clients feel dissatisfied with awards.

The FOS and BBRS will only consider cases where financial products are involved. In cases where markers are loaded by telecommunication companies, the Communications Ombudsman[74] will not deal with complaints relating

71 *Churchill v Merthyr Tydfil County Borough Council* [2023] EWCA Civ 1416

72 Judgment is a legal term, as opposed to the spelling of the word 'judgement'

73 There are very limited circumstances in which FOS will order the payment of costs, but since it offers a free service, costs for applying to FOS for it to review a decision will be disregarded

74 See www.ombudsman-services.org/sectors/communications

to fraud. The line of appeal in such telecommunication cases would be to the organisation first, then Cifas, failing which the courts.

Those Subjects loaded to Cifas' Internal Fraud Database also do not have a right of appeal to the FOS because the marker does not relate to a financial product. In their cases, unless the organisations are persuaded to remove the markers voluntarily, the only line of appeal would be to Cifas and, failing that, through the Employment Tribunal.

The scope for injustice to be caused by organisations loading markers incorrectly – or being uncooperative when challenged – is obvious. Better transparency about these systems and fraud awareness education are important to help ensure that people take better care of their data, become more security wise, and are diverted away from agreeing to act in a criminal way; this is particularly relevant to the government's desire to tackle the money mule problem.

2 The money mule problem

The Cifas fraud database and marker system is utilised to identify, disrupt, and prevent money launderers from accessing mainstream banking and credit facilities.

The scale of the money laundering problem is enormous. According to the NCA's website:[1]

> Money laundering underpins and enables most forms of organised crime, allowing crime groups to further their operations and conceal their assets. Although there are no exact figures there is a realistic possibility that the scale of money laundering impacting the UK economy is in the hundreds of billions of pounds.

This is supported by a 2023 study which suggested that fraud could cost the UK economy £219 billion a year.[2] There are some suggestions that nearly 40% of the world's dirty money goes through the City of London[3] and British Crown dependencies.[4]

This book does not provide the space to cover the history of money laundering in detail; many other authors have written comprehensively about it. The world has become a very different place since the days of the Cragg Vale Coiners; the audacious 'King' David Hartley and his cohort of West Yorkshire weavers and farm workers who capsized the British economy in the 1760s by shaving and then milling the offcuts of genuine coins, flooding the economy

1 See www.nationalcrimeagency.gov.uk

2 See Annual Fraud Indicator 2023 report, published by Crowe, Peters &Peters and University of Portsmouth www.pdacounterfraud.co.uk/wp-content/uploads/2024/01/The-Financial-Cost-of-Fraud-2023-Crowe-University-of-Portsmouth.pdf

3 'The City of London' and 'The City' is reference to the Square Mile, the banking heart of London, and the financial organisations that have operated from there. It is equivalent to Wall Street in New York.

4 See www.theguardian.com/world/article/2024/may/14/nearly-40-of-dirty-money-is-laundered-in-london-and-uk-crown-dependenies

DOI: 10.4324/9781003588542-2

with fake currency.[5] A good place to start to understand its modern history and the scale of the issues involved is Oliver Bullough's excellent book, *Butler To The World; How Britain became the servant of tycoons, tax dodgers, kleptocrats and criminals*[6] in which he also helpfully explains the differences between the US and UK regulators. Other books worth reading include Jeffrey Robinson's *The laundrymen: inside money laundering, the world's third largest business*[7] and Tom Burgis' *Kleptopia; How Dirty Money Is Conquering The World.*[8] However, none of these mention the vital role fraud markers play in combatting and disrupting financial crime. Robinson can be forgiven since his book was written in the 1990s; Bullough and Burgis may not have been aware of their existence.

Anti-money laundering legislation was ostensibly developed to combat two key threats: kleptocracy[9] and criminals laundering the proceeds of crime. There is crossover between the two.

This book is not meant to be political. The following criticism of banking practices and the Conservative party[10] is an unavoidable consequence of the Subject matter of the next two chapters. The fraud marker system makes a lot of sense when you understand how day-to-day personal customer and business banking practices relate to the wider issues surrounding money laundering, particularly kleptocracy. It is also difficult to explain the reasoning behind the systems and processes used today without understanding the historical context behind them. There has been a positive but forced change in attitudes over the past few years. The systems used – and their potential adverse and positive impacts –are Subject to parliamentary rather than political scrutiny in the UK.

Since the 1950s the City of London has enabled criminals and oligarchs to hide their ill-gotten gains. I agree with Bullough's historical notion of the British banking system acting as a butler, an enabler, acting on the basis that 'if we don't allow this someone else will'.

There is a correlation between the way in which governments tax their populations and how governments have allowed kleptocrats to launder their ill-gotten gains. It is easier for governments to tax a population which has no option but to pay tax, such as employees through the UK's Pay As

5 Recommended reading 'The Gallows Pole', Benjamin Myers, Bloomsbury ISBN 978-1-52 66-1115-4

6 Profile Books ISBN 9781788165884

7 Arcade Publishing ISBN 9781559703857

8 WilliamsCollinsbooks.com ISBN 978-0-00-830838-4

9 A Kleptocrat is defined by the Cambridge Dictionary as 'a leader who makes himself or herself rich and powerful by stealing from the rest of the people'.

10 The Conservative Party is a political party in the UK that from 2010 until 1 July 2024 formed the government.

You Earn (PAYE)[11] system operated by employers, than to take direct action against billionaires and corporations seeking to reduce their exposure to tax through creative accounting and self-assessment, historically leaving the oligarchs[12] and kleptocrats with almost free reign to continue their nefarious and profitable activities. It was not until Russia invaded Ukraine that the Conservative party was forced to revisit its well-reported political connections and relationships with kleptocrats.

It could be argued that Cifas positioned itself as the go-to fraud database that the UK banks could conveniently use to demonstrate compliance with their ever-increasing regulatory duties, particularly relating to their reporting duties to the NCA and AML compliance functions. A cynic may say that the banks initially saw the benefit of using such fraud databases to throw the regulators off the scent of the kleptocrats, oligarchs and serious players in the laundromat business that have made the banks billions of pounds worth of profits, by focusing compliance on the millions of average business and personal customers.

Proof of banks previous failures to tackle serious criminality is well reported, as just a few select examples demonstrate. At the end of 2021, NatWest[13] was rightly fined £264.8 million for historic offences of failing to comply with anti-money laundering regulations. Although found not be not complicit in the actual laundering of money, the sentencing judge at Southwark Crown Court,[14] Mrs Justice Cockerill, considered that the Bank was functionally vital in allowing it to take place, criticising NatWest's failings without which the money could not have been laundered.[15] The FCA which brought the prosecution discovered that NatWest's employees had handled vast amounts of cash through 50 of its branches. A firm of jewellers in Bradford, Fowler Oldfield, which had a reported turnover of £15 million, had deposited £365 million over five years in its NatWest accounts, of which £264 million was in cash. Despite being warned by other employees about what was happening, the bank's fraud investigation team had failed to investigate.

Around that time, HSBC[16] was fined £63.95 million for poor AML and terrorist financing policies between 2000 and 2018. Those sums are almost

11 Pay As You Earn is the system of taxation where employers deduct from employees at source; see www.gov.uk/government/statistics/announcements/earnings-and-employment-from-pay-as-you-earn-real-time-information-uk-april-2025

12 An Oligarchy is a government where power is held by a small number of powerful people; an Oligarch is a supporter or member of such a system; see www.merriam-webster.com/dictionary/oligarch.

13 NatWest refers to National Westminster Bank PLC www.natwest.com

14 The Crown Court is where the most serious criminal cases are heard.

15 See www.theguardian.com/business/2021/dec/13/natwest-fined-264m-after-admitting-breaching-anti-money-laundering-rules

16 HSBC refers to HSBC UK Plc www.hsbc.co.uk

chickenfeed[17] compared to the $1.9 billion HSBC was fined by bank regulators in the United States in 2012 after it admitted it had handled billions of dollars of drugs money for the notorious Mexican drug lord and cartel[18] operator, El Chapo.[19] It was reported that HSBC had moved $670 billion from Mexico alone (much of that likely to be attributed to El Chapo), itself small fry to the more than $200 trillion of funds it had moved without adequate anti-money laundering controls over a three-year period, putting into context how much money it made from such nefarious practices.[20]

The fines imposed in the UK are small compared to the deep level of fines imposed in the United States. The fascinating, eye opening, and utterly damning *Violation Tracker* blog[21] lists the cases brought by the US regulators and through litigation in the US courts. Globally firms were fined nearly $5 billion in 2022 for breaching anti-money laundering regulations, of which Danske bank was the recipient of a $2.1 billion fine in the US. But in the UK fines fell from $436.5 million in 2021 to $188.2 million the following year, of which $132 million was imposed against Santander. The FCA issued 14 fines that year, compared to just four in 2021.[22]

The cynic may therefore be justified in thinking that the UK has been unwilling to bite off the hand that feeds it. There is evidence that supports this. Burgis reported in his book a fascinating exchange between the then Chancellor of the Exchequer,[23] George Osborne and the Head of the Federal Reserve,[24] Ben Bernanke and the US Treasury Secretary, Tim Geithner, to ask for leniency for British banks accused of money laundering. Osborne was apparently concerned that there was a risk to the financial stability to the economy if banks were convicted in the United States, where convicted banks are banned from dealing in dollars.[25]

Is this why banks tread a tightrope with the US regulators, whereas in the UK they are seemingly treated gently by comparison? It may explain why in the UK the banks themselves are never prosecuted, instead being dealt with by

17 Chickenfeed means an amount of money that is so low in comparison to others that it is unimportant can be ignored; see www.dictionary.cambridge.org/dictionary/english/chickenfeed

18 Cartel in this context means a criminal organisation composed of independent drug lords who collude with each other to improve their profits and dominate illegal trade; see www.en.wikipedia.org/wiki/Drug_cartel

19 See www.inews.co.uk/news/long-reads/hsbc-money-laundering-scandal-why-no-banker-jail-1700793

20 www.gfintegrity.org/press-release/money-laundering-and-hsbc-how-it-affects-you/

21 www.violationtracker.goodjobsfirst.org

22 See www.cityam.com/financial-crime-anti-money-laundering-and-crypto-fines-surge-to-4bn-in-regulatory-crackdown/?amp=1

23 The Chancellor of the Exchequer is the UK Government's chief financial minister

24 The Federal Reserve (otherwise known as 'The Fed') is the Central Bank of the United States of America and carries out a similar function to the Bank of England in the UK

25 Burgis pages 170–171

regulatory fines? Does this explain why the FCA seemingly has done so little to enforce regulations against banks, and why the recent enforcement action is based on historic breaches? For example, in December 2022 Santander was fined £107.8 million (the $132 million referred to earlier) for failures in its AML procedures dating back to 2015.[26] Why is it taking the FCA so long to take enforcement action? There are not any up-to-date published statistics of banks current AML procedure performance. This issue was commented upon by the House of Lords in its *Breaking the Chain* report. It is worth considering the comment at point 209 of the report which reads:

> The FCA told us that it 'prolifically enforced' the AML regime. Since 2018 it has taken action against 11 firms for inadequate AML, anti-bribery and corruption controls, culminating in £655 million in penalties. Far from being 'prolific', this figure seems startlingly low.

The House of Lords' reasoning can be explained in part by the fact that the FCA is funded out of the fees it charges regulated firms. Perhaps it should charge those firms more to increase its budget in line with the funds available to the US regulator, The Securities and Exchange Commission (SEC),[27] which receives its funding from Congress? In 2023 the SEC's budget was $2.99 billion.[28] By comparison the FCA's budget for 2023/2024 was £664.4 million.[29] Or perhaps FCA funding should, as in the US, be provided by the State? In September 2024, the *Financial Times* reported 11 successful prosecutions for financial crimes in the previous 12 months, compared to just one the previous year, with another 21 being charged. It was also reported that there had been a significant recruitment drive but only £35.5 million had been collected in fines compared to £212.6 million the previous year.[30]

But, without the interference of politicians, the City of London cannot control overseas regulators. It is arguable that the development of the Financial Action Task Force (FATF),[31] which has standardised anti-money laundering measures around the globe, has resulted in the British banks and their offshore offshoots gradually having no choice but to be seen to act against money laundering, in the process weakening the political grasp over them.

26 www-dailymail-co-uk.cdn.ampproject.org/c/s/www.dailymail.co.uk/news/article-11519981/amp/Santander-UK-fined-107-8M-Financial-Conduct-Authority-money-laundering-controls.html

27 The Securities and Exchange Commission is the US financial regulator which carries out similar functions to the FCA in the UK

28 www.usaspending.gov/agency/securities-and-exchange-commission?fy=2023

29 www.fca.org.uk/publications/business-plans/2023-24

30 Reported on 5th September 2024 by The Financial Times www.ft.com/content/4b5bf285-ee34-4f43-be1e-1db9a7f5b1b8

31 See www.fatf-gafi.org/en/home.html

The FATF has a particular interest in combatting kleptocracy, and as alluded to earlier, kleptocrats have oiled the British economy for decades, enabled by political desire which has reduced regulatory requirements to enable The City of London to compete with Wall Street[32] and beyond. The FCA references FATF guidelines on PEPs and high-risk countries.[33]

In the UK, banks and other regulated organisations are supposed to issue SARs to the NCA when they suspect money laundering. If anybody fails to report suspected money laundering, then they commit a criminal offence. This law applies to individuals as well as professionals. Self-reporting provides a defence to failing to report. The only exceptions to this rule are for lawyers advising those suspected of money laundering[34] and Higher Education Institutions (HEI) such as universities[35] which since they are not part of the Regulated Sector[36] are not 'explicitly included' within the Money Laundering Regulations 2017, although HEI employees and the HEIs themselves could be prosecuted if they deal with criminal property.[37]

The offence of *tipping off*, contrary to Section 330 Proceeds of Crime Act 2002, is committed when a suspect is notified that they have been reported to the police. Many a Solicitor has been struck off the Roll[38] by the Solicitors Regulation Authority (SRA)[39] for doing so and imprisoned. However, there is nothing to prevent banks from questioning suspects before they issue a SAR since the offence is only committed if the suspect is told they have been reported.

Chatham House,[40] otherwise known as the Royal Institute of International Affairs, is a policy institute based in London. Its mission statement is to *help governments and societies build a sustainably secure, prosperous and just*

32 Wall Street, New York; see City of London earlier for its UK equivalent.

33 www.fca.org.uk/firms/money-laundering-terrorist-financing/high-risk-customers-politically-exposed-persons

34 *Bowman v Fels* [2005] EWCA Civ 226

35 See *Higher Education Institutions and the Anti-Money Laundering and Counter-Terrorism Financing Regulations* paper by Professor Nicholas Ryder, Dr Sam Bourton, Demelza Hall and Dr Henry Hillman www.orca.cardiff.ac.uk/id/eprint/160289 Sweet & Maxwell ISSN 0011-135X

36 Regulated sector means organisations which are regulated by the FCA or others such as the Solicitors Regulation Authority.

37 See www.opendemocracy.net/en/dark-money-investigations/academics-university-transparency-secret-donations-dark-money/

38 The Roll of Solicitors is managed by the Law Society – currently there are more than 150,000 Solicitors on the roll

39 The Solicitors Regulation Authority regulates solicitors in England and Wales. Solicitors are lawyers who practice non-contentious transactional work, typically company law, conveyancing (real estate), and probate but also practice litigation, family law, and criminal law in the lower courts, and if they have 'Higher Rights of Audience' they may also appear in the Higher Courts. Solicitors generally instruct counsel (see 'barrister' later) to appear in the Higher Courts when they do not have or wish to exercise 'Higher Rights of Audience' or where expert specialist advice is required to assist with a case; see www.sra.org.uk

40 See www.chathamhouse.org

world. On 8 December 2021 it published a report: *The UK's kleptocracy problem*[41] which highlights several issues which are of particular concern to UK banking and its anti-money laundering regime. It reported that the post-Soviet elite were enabled by British organisations providing professional services to enhance their clients' reputations and launder money for them. It commented that the UK relied on private professional services such as lawyers, estate agents, and accountants to carry out AML checks, but there were inconsistencies because whilst the banking and finance sector had become risk averse and was overzealous in reporting suspicious activities, the professional service providers tended to under report. It also highlighted the failure of the NCA to investigate and enforce; it criticised and put forward both flawed reasoning and lack of appetite to oppose rigorous legal challenges by suspects as deterring regulators' attempts to prosecute PEPs. The obvious hole in the system is the fact that the NCA is under resourced. Chatham House reported the NCA only has 120 officers tasked with dealing with more than 577,000 annual reports. The NCA struggles to keep and recruit officers mainly because the banks themselves need well-trained, experienced investigators and pay premiums the NCA cannot match. Given the vast number of SARs that are sent to it, there is an obvious disconnect between the NCA's ability to investigate cases and its desire and duty to do so. The problem was exacerbated when sanctions were imposed on so called Russian Oligarchs in response to Russia's invasion of the Ukraine. Chatham House also commented on the use of aggressive reputation management including actions for libel, use of public relations and quasi-defamation cases, and reputation laundering such as through donations to universities. The Conservative party was considered as being open to the influence of wealthy donors originating from post-Soviet era kleptocracies.

A cynic may think that by deliberately underfunding the NCA and police resources assigned to investigate money laundering, the Conservative Government sought to enable the City of London and its kleptocrat friends to enrich themselves and each other. A good example of how kleptocracy works in practice was reported by the BBC in May 2023[42] which described the NCA's investigation into Javad Marandi, who just so happened to be a donor of the Conservative Party.

A cynic may also think that the Conservative Government's decision to deregulate the banking industry again was another vaguely guarded attempt to protect the City of London and shore up post-Brexit inward investment. Crown dependencies such as The British Virgin Islands have long played host to – and enabled – the international movement of dirty money, and Britain's relationship with such enablers was threatened by greater integration into the European Economic Community.

41 www.chathamhouse.org/2021/12/uks-kleptocracy-problem
42 See www.bbc.co.uk/news/uk-61264369

When professional service providers take on a new client, they must undertake rigorous client on-boarding processes, ascertaining whether the client is connected to – or is themselves – a PEP. If a client is considered a PEP, then permission must be granted by the firm's Money Laundering Reporting Officer (MLRO) before the firm can agree to act. The PEP system is therefore designed to identify those who may be considered a risk of enabling kleptocracy.

There is no international definition of a PEP; the FATF's description of it is commonly used as a starting point. Broadly speaking, PEPs fall into three categories: foreign PEPs; domestic PEPs; and those who have a prominent function within state owned enterprises or international organisations. To be classified as a domestic or foreign PEP individuals such as heads of state or government, senior public officials, those with senior positions in the judiciary and military, senior executives of state-owned corporations, and high-profile political figures will fall under review. Family members or close associates of PEPs also fall into the PEP status. In the UK the FCA stipulates that enhanced due diligence is applied when dealing with PEPs. Other organisations, such as the SRA, also provide similar advice to their members. Measures include conducting enhanced due diligence when business relationships are established and ongoing monitoring of the relationships formed with PEPs. Banks are less likely to take the risk of going against the automated processes when they face prosecution themselves, and consequently they will become even more risk averse. In 2023 numerous high-profile politicians in the UK complained that they had been debanked as part of due diligence and PEP checks.[43] The FCA investigated but found no evidence that banks were politically biased, as had been alleged. That review led to a politically expedient change in the law whereby the UK PEPs were considered 'inherently lower risk' than foreign PEPs[44] with provision made by section 77 of the Financial Services and Markets Act 2023 to amend Part 3 of the Money Laundering and Terrorist Financing (Information on the Payer) Regulations 2017.[45] The government press release stated 'Banks occupy a privileged place in society, and it is right that we fairly balance the rights of banks to act in their commercial interest, with the right for everyone to express themselves freely'. Further guidance and a consultation were issued by the FCA on the treatment of PEPs.[46]

Risk appetite is an essential part of any decision to de-bank a customer. Banking is a matter of trust and confidence, and terms and conditions are broad allowing financial organisations to close accounts for a variety of reasons.

43 See www.standard.co.uk/business/business-news/ordinary-people-offered-no-lifeline-in-debanking-scandal-says-lawyer-b1105187.html and many other articles on the Subject
44 See www.gov.uk/government/news/government-clamps-down-on-unfair-bank-account-closures
45 SI 2017/692
46 See www.fca.org.uk/news/press-releases/FCA-calls-on-firms-to-improve-treatment-of-PEPs

The failure of customers to comply with requests for information is a frequent cause of de-banking, particularly when banks are under regulatory and compliance pressure from regulators.[47]

Away from kleptocrats, criminals need bank accounts to clean their ill-gotten money. A sophisticated criminal industry has been born to service that money by creating and using mule accounts. Criminals, such as sex or human traffickers, drugs dealers, arms dealers, terrorists and the like, need to clean their ill-gotten gains to legitimise their money. That money needs to get into mainstream banking where it is then transferred into legitimate investments such as property or less legitimate forms of investment such as cryptocurrencies.

I do not like the traditional, academic, definition of the way money laundering works: placement, layering and integration. It is too formulaic; the definitions of each phase are too long winded and theoretical. I much prefer Nigel Morris-Cotterill's terminology of 'hiding, moving and investing' which is much simpler to understand.[48] In practice money laundering is nuanced and is designed to be deceptive; the people behind it are very devious. I have seen many different and clever ways in which money laundering operates, and even experienced counter-fraud professional sometimes find it difficult to spot. In very simplistic terms, bank accounts act as washing machines for money launderers: dirty money goes in, washes around, and when it is removed it is clean. The problem criminals have is that they need lots of bank accounts to do this, and they concoct clever solutions to ensure that they can successfully launder their money before cashing it out. Mule accounts are commonly part of complex transaction chains, with several intermediary accounts used to reduce the risk of the fraudulent funds being detected, dissipating the funds into smaller transactions making them more difficult to trace.

In an excellent article published by *Reuters*[49] on 14 October 2021 entitled 'Welcome to Britain the bank scam capital of the world',[50] Lawrence White and Ian Withers wrote that Britain was the global epicentre for scammers purchasing consumers' personal details on the dark web. It is the UK's super-fast payments infrastructure and light policing of fraud which led to this situation. Per capita the fraud rate in the UK is triple that of the United States. They reported how the FPS has facilitated faster fraud and that criminals were exploiting the digitalisation of banking. Automated bot attacks were increasing, where criminals were using stolen identity to overrun websites, setting up new accounts or accessing existing ones.

47 See www.reuters.com/world/uk/uk-inquiry-finds-banks-shut-142000-small-business-accounts-year-2024-02-27/

48 Create Space Independent Publishing Platform 'How Not To Be A Money Launderer: The Avoidance of Money Laundering and Fraud in your Organisation' ISBN-13 978-1467971225

49 Reuters, an international news agency; see www.reuters.com

50 See www.reuters.com/world/uk/welcome-britain-bank-scam-capital-world-2021-10-14/

A key area where money laundering is rife is in cryptocurrency transactions. A generation of young people have felt empowered by cryptocurrency. They believe they are financially independent when they invest in it, seemingly making money easily with little effort, believing it attractive compared to making money through diligent labour. However, they often fall victim to cunning criminals. I have seen many scams started by 'gurus' posting on social media such as Instagram, Snap Chat or WhatsApp, offering opportunities to join groups and learn how to trade. These are cleverly orchestrated. *Which*? reported that cryptocurrency scams had increased 34% between November 2020 and December 2021, with *Action Fraud* reporting it had received 9,458 complaints. The losses were huge, £204.5 million, at an average loss of £21,620.[51]

I have seen banks miss many mule transactions before finally spotting tell-tale signs of money laundering; with experience they are getting better at highlighting such accounts. Some banks such as Santander limit how much its customers can invest in crypto-currency, and others such as Monzo state in their terms and conditions that they will not support certain crypto exchanges such as Binance. Barclays does have a relationship with Coinbase to provide a faster payments service but nothing else. According to its terms and conditions Revolut allows certain cryptocurrencies to be paid into its accounts. However, after Revolut joined Cifas in 2022 I soon saw Subjects marked who had been trading cryptocurrencies. These markers were either due to fraudulent funds being identified to it by reporting banks or complaints made against its customers by reporting banks claiming that their customers had not received their cryptocurrencies. Fraudulent funds are rife within the blockchains.[52] Transfers made through the blockchain can be fraught with danger since customers are unlikely to know the real identity of the people they are dealing with. The transfers take place between individuals; the exchanges hold the cryptocurrency in escrow until the seller has confirmed they have received their funds. In that way the exchanges have traditionally argued that they can avoid AML compliance procedures, which in turn is an attractive proposition to criminals. In practice sellers need to take extraordinary care to ensure they identify who they are transacting with, but even so they cannot guarantee they will be safe. Neither can sellers be sure where their customers are based since cryptocurrency is an international commodity. A detailed analysis of how cryptocurrency fraud operates highlights that the US, Russia and Nigeria are the 'largest players in Bitcoin transactions globally'.[53] The often-repeated warning 'never share you bank details with anyone' is made for very good reason!

51 See www.which.co.uk/policy-and-insight/article/young-people-most-likely-to-report-being-scammed-amid-dramatic-rise-in-fraud-which-finds-amd2W2I1MciU

52 'Block chain' see www.investopedia.com/terms/b/blockchain.asp

53 Garba, K. H., Lazarus, S., & Button, M. (2024). An assessment of convicted cryptocurrency fraudsters. *Current Issues in Criminal Justice*, 1–17. https://doi.org/10.1080/10345329.2024.2403294

The characters who established the blockchains[54] are sometimes dubious, such as Sam Bankman-Fried – the founder of FTX who earned 25 years in prison for defrauding his customers[55] – or Changpeng Zho, the founder of Coinbase who probably feels lucky to have only been sentenced to four months imprisonment for violating anti-money laundering regulations.[56] The Ponzi[57] scheme otherwise known as One Coin needs little introduction.[58] In early 2023 I was signposted to a report on the UK government's website[59] which revealed that in December 2022 Coinbase, Inc. (the Applicant) was applying to change the name of the respondent, COINBASE LIMITED, a company registered with Companies House under number 13237380, which it accused of being a front for fraudulent scammer type activities via a website, BITCOINBASELIMITED.COM. The applicant claimed that the primary respondent was 'blocking the applicant from using the same company name; misleading consumers into believing the applicant and the company are connected; perpetrating fraud or phishing schemes on the public'. The defence put forward by the respondent was extraordinary. It claimed that the applicant had stolen Coinbase Inc from the co-respondent, Mr Stephen Mollah, 'which was hijacked from him by an international group who invaded his house'. Mr Mollah claimed – but could not prove – that he was the inventor of Bitcoin, Mr Satoshi Nakamoto.[60] Mr Mollah claimed in his defence that: 'he created the word Coinbase in 2007 and has used it ever since he created it for his Bitcoin and Blockchain technology project, which he planned to launch anonymously'. He also claimed that he designed the Coinbase Exchange to trade his Bitcoin in 2009 and that when he invented the Bitcoin mining technology and the Blockchain Ledger, he created Coinbase to store all his mined Bitcoins. Mr Mollah also claimed that the applicant was not the owner of Coinbase Inc., and he had a pending case in the UK High Court[61] against the applicant and the organised international group, and Mr Mollah denied the accusations of fraud and stated that his company did not have a website. He claimed that a secret group had registered numerous fraudulent web domains using his company's name and his registered address to create a false image of himself and

54 'Block chain' see www.investopedia.com/terms/b/blockchain.asp

55 See www.nytimes.com/2024/03/28/technology

56 See www.nytimes.com/2024/04/30/technology/binance-founder-changpeng-zhao-sentenced.html

57 Well known fraudster; see *Action Fraud* website earlier

58 See www.justice.gov/usao-sdny/pr/co-founder-multi-billion-dollar-cryptocurrency-pyramid-scheme-onecoin-pleads-guilty

59 See www.gov.uk/government/publications/company-names-tribunal-decision-coinbase-limited/decision-on-coinbase-limited

60 For further reading on this mysterious figure see www.forbes.com/advisor/investing/cryptocurrency/who-is-satoshi-nakamoto/

61 High Court is reference to the High Court of England and Wales which considers the highest value and most technical civil cases.

he suspected that the applicant was behind this. The court found in favour of the applicant, ruling that Mr Mollah's claims that there was a UK High Court case where he was the applicant were unsupported and that Mr Mollah had provided no evidence that he was in fact Mr Nakamoto. The court ruled that none of (several) defences the respondent put forward could be relied upon and ordered that Coinbase Limited should change its name within one month of the order dated 8 December 2022.

In April 2022 the Conservative Government revealed plans to make the UK a 'global cryptoassets hub', bringing stablecoins within regulation, creating a 'financial market initiative sandbox to help firms innovate', exploring ways to enhance the UK's competitive tax system to encourage further development of the market and establish a 'Crypto Asset Engagement Group' to work with the Royal Mint[62] on a Non-Fungible Token.[63]

In November 2022, the *Financial Times* produced a film called *Can crytpo be controlled?*[64] which set out the problems ahead for regulating cryptocurrencies. Until regulation occurs, mainstream banking is likely to see cryptocurrency as an unacceptable money laundering risk. The fact that exchanges such as Binance have been reluctant to impose even basic AML checks on customers have done their reputations no favours. In July 2024 the FCA fined CB Payments Limited, which is part of Coinbase's group of companies, £3.5 million for 'significant weaknesses and gaps in the Firm's financial crime control network' which included on-boarding 'high-risk' customers.[65] Some cryptocurrencies arrive and depart with alarming and suspicious speed. But is that tarnished reputation not also the fault of the fraudsters and money launderers who use cryptocurrency rather than the platforms themselves which are transparent and therefore relatively easy to investigate if you have the technology and training? Government would be deluded to assume that regulated crypto-currency will create automatic buy-in from the banks.

In some circumstances banks use assumptions when making decisions to block accounts. For example, many people wishing to move Naira, the national currency of Nigeria, out of that country and into the UK are caught by British banks automatically blocking transactions and loading Cifas markers. The reason for that is because in 2016 the Nigerian government suspended the transfer of Naira through unregulated International Money Transfer Organisations (IMTOs).[66] It meant that only US dollars could be transferred out of

62 The Royal Mint is the organisation which produces UK currency notes and coins; see www.royalmint.com

63 www.gov.uk/government/news/government-sets-out-plan-to-make-uk-a-global-cryptoasset-technology-hub

64 www.youtube.com/watch?v=CVsYMVHW17c

65 www.fca.org.uk/publication/final-notices/cb-payments-limited-2024.pdf

66 See www.monitor.icef.com/2016/03/nigeria-tightens-foreign-exchange-controls-to-limit-use-for-study-abroad/

Nigeria and only safely through recognised regulated IMTOs such as Western Union Transfer.[67] It was part of the Nigerian's government's attempts to get its country off the FATF's grey list; at the time of writing Nigeria is still on it but has demonstrated a commitment to improving its procedures. Regrettably, the Nigerian economy, financial system, and government have been historically riddled with fraud and corruption. In 2023, the Nigerian Intelligence Unit published guidance, the 'National Inherent Risk Assessment of Money Laundering in Nigeria',[68] to mitigate money laundering; it is hoped that the proposed measures are successful and help improve Nigeria's reputation globally. As Garba, Lazarus, and Button's article explains, only 36.8% of adult Nigerians have access to banking, a fact that has resulted in widespread use of cryptocurrency.

There are many cultures where money lending and exchanging between friends and contacts is common. Such cultures have laudable traditions where family members will seek to support each other, either by sending money back home or when members of their families come to the UK to study or work. The recent collapse in the value of the Naira prompted many Nigerian students to fail to pay for their university course fees; many will have been supported by their families at home.[69] In Nigeria, and other countries, unregulated money exchange bureaus pass the bank details of those that have engaged them to other parties to then send the money to the UK bank accounts. The source of funds is therefore obscure and, experience has told banks, possibly fraudulent.

There is a moral dilemma, one which divides opinions. In my experience some money mules are themselves victims, used by clever, devious criminals to facilitate the laundering of criminal property. This is now recognised by the police. The UK Financial Intelligence Unit (UKFIU) *SARS in Action*[70] report helpfully defines the roles within money muling as either 'witting' or 'unwitting'. Witting money mules can be complicit, or negligent and naïve such as where they have not received 'assurances or credible cover stories regarding the source of funds'. Unwitting money mules can be the victims of fraud, such as romance or employment frauds, those who are coerced or threatened, or those who have been the victim of identity theft or where fake accounts are created using false identification. However, many banks have taken a more stringent view and have marked anybody they suspect of being a money mule, whether witting or unwitting.

During the global COVID-19 pandemic there was a rapid rise in the amount of alleged money mule activity. Here is a classic example I have seen countless times. A young person (usually stuck away from home due to lock

67 www.westernunion.com
68 See www.nfiu.gov.ng/Home/NiraReports
69 See www.bbc.co.uk/news/articles/c888926qx58o
70 Issue 20, May 2023 see www.nationalcrimeagency.gov.uk/who-we-are/publications/649-sars-in-action-issue-20/file

down conditions and struggling for money) would see a message on Snapchat offering them the opportunity to make easy money. Intrigued, the young person would send a message of interest. A conversation would then flow with the young person being told that the opportunity was to learn about 'trading'. Obviously young people like to make money, and many feel empowered with a feeling of independence when they think they can make a living easily. Those feelings are secured when the transaction they are asked to perform looks legitimate. In this instance, young people were asked to download an App called Luno. They were then asked to provide their newfound friend with their bank details. They were then told to send £1 to an account, just to check that their account was working. They were then told to wait for instructions. A few days later a message would appear on the Luno App asking them to transfer some money they had just received in their account to another account. Then one of two things happened: either they received a message from their bank that their account had been blocked; or they moved the money as requested. Sometimes several transactions took place before the young person's account was blocked. As soon as they had their accounts blocked, they would try to message their newfound friend only to discover that they had disappeared from trace and had also been blocked from contacting them. When they spoke to their bank to find out what had gone on, their bank asked for evidence of the conversations. Unfortunately, the young person then discovered that they had not kept screen shots of the messages, and because Snapchat messages disappear after 24 hours, they had no evidence to support their contention that they had been scammed, and if messages had been saved then they may have been incomplete or lacked context. The banks refused to reopen the accounts and our young person, who might be studying for a degree in accountancy or banking and finance, found that they were marked on the Cifas database for up to six years and their promising career was on the buffers before it had even started.

I am frequently contacted by people reporting that accounts have been set up in their names without their knowledge. Inconsistencies in the approach taken by banks to such appeals have become apparent. For example, Wayne (not his real name) had three markers loaded against him by Skipton Building Society,[71] Nationwide,[72] and Santander[73] for 'false application fraud'. He proved that he had left some personal documents at home when it was being renovated by builders only to discover that a secured room had been broken into. The stolen details were used to apply for bank accounts. Santander refused to remove the marker despite the evidence and arguments being the same as to the other two which agreed to remove the markers they had loaded.

71 Skipton Building Society; see www.skipton.co.uk
72 Nationwide refers to Nationwide Building Society, www.nationwide.co.uk
73 Santander refers to Santander UK PLC; see www.santander.co.uk

Impersonation, where friends and family are tricked or have their data and identities stolen through malware or hacking, is a huge problem and is another common theme in the cases I see. Such activity amounts to facility takeover, in 2022 accounting for 11% of cases reported to the Cifas database. In 2020 Cifas reported 17,000 such cases involving people aged between 21 and 30.

Cash is also important for the money launderer, as the NatWest case mentioned earlier reveals. In another example in the UK, the Post Office was implicated in enabling cash-based money laundering (CBML) by a regulated FCA payment services provider, Beltcastle. The modus operandi was for Beltcastle to collect cash, take it to the Post Office which would deposit the money into bank accounts managed by Santander among others, and in so doing would return funds to the customers. It was a classic money laundering operation involving £1.3 billion of illicit funds.[74]

Many people are persuaded into doing a favour for friends, such as those who are having difficulty with their bank account but have money coming in that they cannot access. Would they mind accepting the money into their bank account and withdrawing the money in cash? Of course, why not help a friend in need? Sometimes the friend offers a small percentage as a thank you, sometimes it is treated as a favour. Some are persuaded at the school gate, escorted to their local bank branch to withdraw cash or encouraged to open a new account specifically for the use of the fraudsters. All such activity is considered money laundering.

Fraudsters target the naïve and vulnerable. Many young people, desperate to make a living, are easy prey of fake job adverts, commonly advertising for 'money transfer agents'. To be paid, the applicant has to provide their bank details. In many cases the 'employee' is asked to forward funds to another account.

Older people are also targeted, particularly through identity fraud where business bank accounts are established with their details.

People selling items online, giving their bank account details to customers rather than using payment gateways such as PayPal, become easy prey for criminals. Fraudsters commonly use 'chargebacks' to commit fraud or launder the proceeds of crime.[75] Although chargebacks are an important mechanism for helping to protect consumers, chargebacks are also open to abuse by fraudsters. People can and do attempt to obtain goods for free. There is a difference between a chargeback and a refund. A buyer should negotiate with the merchant for a refund in the first instance. But, if a buyer suspects an unauthorised charge has been made to their account; or goods have not been delivered; or goods were defective and the merchant refuses to refund; or

74 See www.acaglobal.com/insights/car-washes-motels-now-post-office-money-laundering-hits-uk-high-street

75 See www.chargebacks911.com for a full explanation.

the items purchased were not those described by the merchant; or the wrong order was received or paid more than was agreed, then the banks may grant a chargeback request. The system operates in reverse too because a person who makes a false chargeback request is likely to receive a Cifas marker.

In response to the money-laundering threat, the counter-fraud profession has seemingly become a boom industry out of necessity. The government employs 10,000 people in counter-fraud roles,[76] and NatWest employs 5,000 people to combat financial crime.[77] Given there are 300 member organisations of UK Finance,[78] the numbers are considerable.

Following on from the House of Lord's Breaking the Chain report, the government proposed to slow down faster payments. Such a decision is a practical and commendable way of deterring fraudulent activity and money muling. Time is important for banks because slowing down transactions means they can investigate more thoroughly instead of potentially rushing decisions, missing criminal activity. This is particularly so in relation to Authorised Push Payment (APP) fraud, where commonly older people, vulnerable to being scammed over the phone, are told that their bank account is not safe and that they need to move all their funds into another account or into cryptocurrency. Banks will compensate victims of APP fraud in some circumstances through the Payment Systems Regulator (PSR).[79] According to UK Finance, in the first half of 2023 £580 million was lost due to such scams.[80]

Time makes it more difficult for criminals as Alexander Wood, a reformed serial fraudster who now assists government and law enforcement to better understand the criminal mindset, explained to me.[81] A certain bank's

> business accounts were a nightmare for us to defraud back in the day, because a new beneficiary cannot be paid until at least one hour after it was added on the system, so we'd have to keep the victim on the phone for ages just talking nonsense before being able to attempt the fraudulent transaction.[82]

On 12 March 2024 the UK government published The Payment Services (Amendment) Regulations 2024[83] to delay payments processing when

76 See www.civil-service-careers.gov.uk/professions/working-in-counter-fraud/#:~:text=There%20are%20over%2010%2C000%20counter%20fraud%20specialists%20working,crime%2C%20leading%20government%20in%20the%20fight%20against%20fraud.

77 www.natwestgroup.com/sustainability/governance-and-responsible-business/detecting-and-preventing-financial-crime.html

78 See www.ukfinance.org.uk

79 www.psr.org.uk/how-we-regulate

80 www.ukfinance.org.uk/news-and-insight/press-release/criminals-steal-over-half-billion-pounds-and-nearly-80-cent-app

81 Quote taken from a conversation direct with Alexander Wood, not attributed to any publication.

82 www.cshub.com/events-anti-financial-crime-summit/speakers/alex-wood

83 assets.publishing.service.gov.uk/media/65eed7233649a26deded630f/Policy_note.pdf

there are reasonable grounds to suspect fraud or dishonesty. The proposed legislation will allow payment service providers to delay outbound payment transactions by up to four business days, only where there are reasonable grounds to believe that someone other than the payer has 'subsequent to fraud or dishonesty perpetrated by someone else'. This is also tied into a reduction of bank liabilities to reimburse the victims of APP fraud from £415,000 to £85,000. This policy appears to contrast with EU proposals to move forward with instant payments. But these regulations, which laudably protect the victims of APP frauds, do however leave customers and banks exposed to high risk in day-to-day transactions.

Out of the thousands of people who have contacted me for advice about fraud markers over the years, the majority have been young people accused of money muling. I always ask them whether they have read their banks' terms and conditions; in that time, I can count the number who have answered 'yes' quite literally on two hands. Very few of them had ever received any education in school about fraud awareness, and most do not know that money laundering is a criminal offence! An example of the risks of not educating students about financial crime and becoming involved in money laundering was laid bare when a sophisticated criminal network was convicted of laundering £55 million after targeting students.[84]

I am aware, from representing young people in Court for many years, that the prime ages for people to commit criminal offences is between the ages of 17 and 24. At that age they are more gullible, more likely to believe as true what adults from experience know to be untrue. But every age range is at risk of falling victim to fraud. Older people are scammed in different ways to young people, but there is crossover, and a common cross-generational theme I see is crypto-currency. Fraud is an issue that crosses the social and economic divide. Rich people are just as likely to fall for scams and mule herders as poor people. For example, many public-school children, some with more disposable income than most people will ever have, are attracted by the entrepreneurial side of cryptocurrency. I have spoken to many young people who feel economically independent, who talk of a feeling of freedom that cryptocurrency dealing provides. Many also like the rush of excitement it provides. Conversely, I have spoken to numerous young people put under pressure at the school gates by older, more sophisticated young adults who groom them into handing over their account details with promises of 'it's legal' and for cash returns.

When those young people go onto university they are at particular risk. Free and financially independent for the first time, making new friends and trusting people who ask them for their account details so they can get some

84 news.met.police.uk/news/local-officers-break-up-ps55m-money-laundering-ring-in-hackney-487319

money through because their account has been blocked or not opened yet (a common threat during freshers' week). But then, come November, they start running out of money and are tempted by offers of cash or the lure of the promised wealth of cryptocurrency trading, or they set up 'side hustles' to sell items online, in each scenario giving away their bank details.

Criminals also target the poor who, struggling to make ends meet during the cost-of-living crisis, offered £100 for their account details and thinking that £100 is the difference between putting food on the table and putting the heating on, take the risk.

Gambling presents an enormous risk to the banking community and its customers, particularly when black market bookmakers are used. Money launderers lay bets off each other, reducing losses and perhaps making some profit, masking the proceeds of crime in the process. In the UK, the Gambling Commission[85] introduced affordability and AML checks which are driving large numbers of punters away from licensed bookmakers.[86] Regrettably this appears to be an example of well-meaning regulation designed to address societal and ethical concerns that is showing signs of backfiring.

So where do we start educating people about fraud risk? The obvious place to start is in schools, because once the younger generations have been taught, they will then pass their knowledge to their parents and grandparents. Much good work is already being done on cyber security awareness. On 1 March 2024, the government announced its action plan to tackle money muling. At its heart is education.[87] One of its stated aims was to work with banks and local authorities to ensure victims are not removed from the banking system and the creation of a post at The Children's Society[88] 'covering money laundering-linked financial exploitation'. There are also several intelligence-based and data sharing proposals within the action plan. But school-aged money mules are only part of the problem because according to Cifas the middle-aged are being targeted in increasing numbers too.[89] Education therefore needs to encompass social, cultural, economic, and age divides. The police and many academics are firmly of the view that appropriate face to face training specifically tailored to the audience is the most effective way of changing attitudes and behaviours. People can be free to discuss issues and ask questions. Follow up through online training with relevant sign posting can follow. Such training does not just empower people to protect themselves from attack; it dissuades those who may have been inclined to criminality.

85 www.gamblingcommission.gov.uk

86 www.racingpost.com/news/gambling-review/new-report-claims-britons-are-staking-up-to-4.3-billion-with-illegal-gambling-operators-every-year-ajm6p1d1ZpCC/

87 See www.gov.uk/government/publications/money-mule-action-plan

88 See www.childrenssociety.org.uk

89 See www.cifas.org.uk/newsroom/middle-aged-mules

Educating people about how the fraud marker systems operate – and the dangers they pose to them, must surely provide a deterrent effect to fraud being committed?

Therefore, there is some justification for the standard of proof in money laundering cases to be below criminal standard given the speed of transactions and the fact that patterns of behaviour can indicate mule operations. The banks are becoming more adept at spotting it quickly. But there are situations where a 'one size fits all' civil standard of proof may not be appropriate, and more discretion needs to be provided by organisations considering appeals against fraud markers.

3 Fraud

The remit for the use of Cifas and other database markers includes flagging where fraud is suspected. When considering why fraud is committed, the mechanism of that decision making is frequently described in Cressey's triangle: *opportunity*, *incentive* and *rationalisation.*[1] That methodology has been taught to counter-fraud and law enforcement professionals who use it daily in their work, but it ignores another essential ingredient: *psychopathy.*[2] Together that framework helps to explain the fraud mindset and much of the following behaviour.

During the COVID-19 pandemic the UK government introduced the Bounce Back Loan Scheme (BBLS). The way in which the banks responded provides an excellent opportunity to comment on the systems and methodology used by banks. The fraud triangle also explains the alleged behaviour of one of the banks that took advantage of the scheme, as will become apparent.

The BBLS was one of the measures the government brought in to help business during 2020. It intended to provide small businesses with quick, easy, and simple access to emergency loans. To ensure swift delivery of such loans, the government reduced the usual fraud checks, turning instead to a system of self-certification. I will summarise how the scheme worked,[3] and in doing so I will highlight some of the issues I saw early in the scheme which have longer term consequences still evident today. I would like to make it clear that many clients told me that were it not for the support provided by the BBLS, their businesses would not have survived the pandemic. However, there are others who in retrospect told me they deeply regretted taking out the loans.

1 corporatefinanceinstitute.com/resources/accounting/fraud-triangle/

2 www.cambridge.org/core/journals/advances-in-psychiatric-treatment/article/psychiatric-and-psychological-aspects-of-fraud-offending/1B192F7E3AE4BAA1ED9BF1BFEA8F7063

3 For full details of the eligibility criteria see www.british-business-bank.co.uk/ourpartners/coronavirus-business-interruption-loan-schemes/bounce-back-loans/faqs-for-small-businesses/#f17

DOI: 10.4324/9781003588542-3

The BBLS was launched on 4 May 2020 by the Department for Business, Energy and Industrial Strategy (BEIS).[4] It offered business loans of between £2,000 and £50,000; the maximum that could be applied for was 25% of annual turnover. The government, through the British Business Bank (BBB), guaranteed 100% for both capital and interest to commercial lenders which in turn would lend the money direct to businesses which were required to repay the debt and interest in full. In other words, if the borrower were to default, then the government would pay the lender the balance of the loan that was due. The loans offered a fixed rate of 2.5% interest over a maximum of ten years, with no capital repayments due in the first year, and with government paying the interest in that first year. The scheme did not require directors to provide personal guarantees. This was a departure from usual practice. Commercial lenders tend to ensure that directors repay loans should their businesses fail to meet their debts, become insolvent or close, by insisting they personally guarantee the debt. In such events the lender can enforce payment of the debt against the guarantor, and if they fail to pay the lender can commence insolvency proceedings against them. As I will explain later, the lack of personal guarantee[5] for Bounce Back Loans is now an area of great concern and is directly relevant to the discussion on fraud markers.

The loan process required the company applicants to self-certify that they would only use the loan for the benefit of the business, not for personal purposes. The rules were slightly different for self-employed applicants because the scheme recognised that the self-employed would, by their very nature, need to rely on the loans to fund their living expenses. This is because companies would pay their staff wages whereas the self-employed do not take a wage, instead they live off profits. Many self-employed/sole trader businesses and start-ups now prefer to do their business as limited companies so the directors can be paid a wage by the company, thereby being able to furlough themselves in times as crisis such as this. There were also no affordability checks in the BBLS, and again the applicant would self-certify their business income or projected income. The applicant would have to self-certify that the business had been adversely affected by COVID-19 and that it was not already insolvent or otherwise a business in difficulty on 31 December 2019. A business in difficulty was defined as a) individuals or companies that have entered into collective insolvency proceedings and b) limited companies which have accumulated losses greater than half of their share capital in their last annual accounts (not applying to SMEs[6] less than three years old). Loans were

4 www.gov.uk/government/organisations/department-for-business-energy-and-industrial-strategy has now been split into three different UK government departments.

5 A personal guarantee is an indemnity provided by a company director or shareholder of a business

6 Small Medium Enterprise – an organisation with fewer than 250 employees and a turnover of less than £50 million

permitted to those who had commenced their business after 1 January 2019 based on projected turnover, again self-certified. Obviously, that caused all sorts of questions and difficulties for start-up businesses, as I will demonstrate in a real-life example later which resulted in Cifas markers being loaded.

There were also rules at that time about only one loan being applicable where there was a group structure of companies. This again caused confusion early on; thankfully the issue was clarified. The original rule was that where businesses were in common ownership only one loan could be applied for; it was changed to allow only one loan if there was a group structure[7] in place. The applicant for a Bounce Back Loan was barred from also applying for the Coronavirus Business Interruption Loan Scheme (CBILS),[8] the Coronavirus Large Business Interruption Loan Scheme (CLBILS),[9] or the Covid Corporate Financing Facility (CCFF)[10] unless those facilities were to be refinanced in full by the Bounce Back Loan. There were also State Aid[11] rules that had to be complied with. Those applicants already Subject to individual voluntary arrangements,[12] debt relief orders, or undischarged bankrupts could not apply.

Confusingly, the application form asked the applicant to confirm that they were not 'an individual other than a sole trader or a partner acting on behalf of a partnership'. I saw several sole traders wrongly accused of making fraudulent applications for Bounce Back Loans, even though another part of the declaration stated: 'I am/we are either a company or limited liability partnership incorporated or established in the UK, or I am/we are tax resident in the UK'. I witnessed misunderstanding of the rules by certain banks or individual assessors assigned to making decisions.

The declaration that had to be signed stated:

> I/We confirm that my/our business was carrying on its business on 1st March 2020, that I was/we are engaged in trading or commercial activity

7 A group company structure is one in which a number of subsidiary companies are controlled by a parent – or holding – company.

8 The Coronavirus Business Interruption Loan Scheme was a UK government-backed scheme that provided loans for SMEs of up to £5 million. The government guaranteed 80% of the loan and deferred interest and payments for 12 months www.gov.uk/guidance/apply-for-the-coronavirus-business-interruption-loan-scheme

9 The Coronavirus Large Business Interruption Scheme was a UK government-backed scheme that provided loans for medium and large businesses of up to £200 million. The government guaranteed 80% of the loan and deferred interest and payments for 12 months www.gov.uk/guidance/apply-for-the-coronavirus-business-interruption-loan-scheme

10 The Covid Corporate Financing Facility provided unsecured loans organisations that made a significant contribution to the UK economy.

11 European Union State Aid rules only allow for government to fund organisations unless it is justified for economic development; see State aid – www.competition-policy.ec.europa.eu/state-aid_en

12 A form of debt repayment plan

> in the United Kingdom as at the date of this application, and that the business has been adversely affected by Covid-19.

There was also a standard fraud declaration:

> I/we recognise that by providing information that is inaccurate or incomplete in any material particular, I/we may be regarded as attempting to gain, or gaining, a financial advantage dishonestly and as such will be liable to criminal prosecution for fraud under the Fraud Act 2006 (or equivalent law in Scotland) (for which penalties include imprisonment or a fine or both), as well as to the forfeiture of all loan proceeds together with interest and court costs,

and 'I/We confirm that the information provided in this application is complete and accurate'.

It did not take long for fraudulent applications for Bounce Bank Loans to be reported by the press. When the *Express* contacted me in November 2020, I was asked to consider and comment on the National Audit Office's report on the BBLS.[13] The National Audit Office had revealed that taxpayers were at risk of losing £26 billion to fraud.[14] The report explained there was a one-month window between the scheme being announced and checks starting to come in. There were various scams where stolen personal details were used to obtain Bounce Back Loans.

I discovered that the scheme was flawed from the outset. In Germany and Switzerland, similar schemes were put together very quickly, before the UK got its act together, and incorporated various safeguards to protect against fraud. Neither Germany nor Switzerland allowed self-certification; neither allowed the payment of dividends from the loans; and neither allowed the loans to be used to repay existing lending. In the UK, no such safeguards were imposed. The government wanted funds to get to businesses within forty-eight hours of application, not the usual four to twelve weeks that such similar commercial finance applications usually took.

Neither the banks themselves nor the intelligence agencies were ready for the launch of the scheme. There was no way of knowing whether duplicate applications had been made, although some training was provided to the banks. In due course, the usual banking safeguards such as Cifas, lender due diligence, and post-accreditation checks came in. Credit checks were used retrospectively; they were not used at the outset because of the self-certification

13 *Express* Newspapers, 5 November 2020; see www.express.co.uk/news/uk/1354256/Rishi-sunak-government-bounce-back-loan-scam-fraud-repayment-BBL-cifas-coronavirus-latest

14 www.nao.org.uk/wp-content/uploads/2020/10/Investigation-into-the-Bounce-Back-Loan-Scheme-Summary.pdf

system. But the reporting system the banks used at that stage, known as the Portal, did not highlight fraud. It was only in March 2022 that it was revealed that the banks had been denied access to independent His Majesty's Revenue and Customs (HMRC)[15] verification for the first eight months of the scheme.[16]

The banks strictly interpreted the definition of 'in business'; they insisted on three months' worth of bank statements to prove that a business was trading on 1 March 2020. The banks ignored various tax law definitions on the subject of 'in business', and other tax-allowed trading or financial relationships were disregarded, as was evidence of business relationships being developed pre-pandemic on a sole-trader basis.

There was also confusion with self-employed/sole trader businesses. The BBB's rules did not mandate that an applicant needed a business account. However, in practice the banks insisted that, before agreeing to provide loans, the applicant had to apply for a business account with them. In that scenario delays were caused, and I saw many businesses apply to different lenders on the BBB's panel before applications for a business account were accepted.

The Insolvency Service[17] was granted extended powers to investigate through The Rating (Coronavirus) and Directors Disqualification (Dissolved Companies) Act 2021. There have been other cases prosecuted by other agencies, notably the Crown Prosecution Service (CPS). It is interesting to note that up to 19 May 2023 there were just six successful prosecutions brought against company directors by the Insolvency Service. In one example the defendant received a six-month prison sentence suspended for 18 months; this related to a £25,000 loan where the company was struck off by the director one week after funds were received and transferred into his personal account. The loan had been repaid in full prior to sentencing.[18] Other prosecutions followed.

Moving back to the issues relating to how Bounce Back Loans were granted, I became aware of a scandal quite early on. Several businesses reported to me that they were encouraged to take out loans they did not actually require. Many who took out loans without needing them at the time faced difficult consequences in due course when interest and payment demands became unaffordable. Some were encouraged to refinance existing debt. At that time, with low interest rates, it made good business sense for the banks

15 His Majesty's Revenue and Customs is the UK government department that collects taxes, see www.gov.uk/government/organisations/hm-revenue-customs

16 See www.belfasttelegraph.co.uk/news/uk/hmrc-denied-banks-access-to-data-that-could-have-prevented-covid-loans-fraud/41449590.html

17 The Insolvency Service is a UK government agency which supports those in financial distress, tackles financial wrongdoing and maximises returns to creditors; see www.gov.uk/government/organisations/insolvency-service

18 See www.gov.uk/government/news/london-businessman-convicted-for-bounce-back-loan-fraud which unfortunately has not reported whether the defendant was disqualified;

to secure their lending against the government. Lord Agnew confirmed what I already knew when, after he resigned his role at the treasury, he reported to the Treasury Committee[19] that, although he supported the BBLS, 'on the fraud side, it was just a Dad's Army operation' and remarked that the operation was a 'joke'. It was reported that the treasury had not used 'an existing counter-fraud database to check loan applicants'; that must be reference to one of the databases, probably Cifas.

Lord Agnew warned that banks would make use of the guarantee to claim money from unpaid loans, choosing to reclaim the funds from government rather trying to recoup the losses themselves. He also reported that he suspected that one of the seven main banks that was involved in the scheme 'really, really took advantage' of it. Although Lord Agnew declined to name the bank in question, from my case load and the issues I uncovered when speaking to clients, I knew it was Starling. It later rigorously denied Lord Agnew's claims to the Treasury Committee that 'They lent indiscriminately . . . they wanted to build their balance sheet. There was no downside because they thought they were going to get the 100% guarantee if any of them [the loans] went wrong'.[20] It later transpired that about 90% of the loans Starling had granted were under the BBLS, many of which defaulted and which caused Starling to be placed under investigation by the FCA.[21]

On 1 May 2023 the *Times* reported about a case that had been decided by the Financial Ombudsman Service.[22] The complaint was that National Westminster Bank PLC (NatWest) told a company director to apply for a Bounce Back Loan when the company was no longer trading. The director was thinking about dissolving the company due to the adverse impact the COVID-19 pandemic had had on it. The Ombudsman referred to correspondence with the director, NatWest, and the company's accountant. The director was either told to – or it was strongly implied that he should – apply for a Bounce Back Loan of £2,000 to cover his company's outstanding overdraft of £300. The application was granted despite the fact the business was not trading and had no income, although it did not fulfil the criteria of 'in difficulty' specified in the application form. Had the business been struck off then the debt would have been written off by the bank. The Ombudsman considered that the director agreed to the loan believing that when the overdraft was cleared NatWest would not block the company from being dissolved. However, when he attempted to strike off the company NatWest refused to allow it due to the

19 See www.bbc.co.uk/news/uk-politics-60681150

20 committees.parliament.uk/oralevidence/9878/html/

21 See www.ft.com/content/c54d039d-48ab-43ff-a9f1-7c4b11872a56

22 See www.thetimes.co.uk/article/natwest-is-censured-over-covid-loan-breach-q02gcms7f – That report is behind a paywall but I was able to identify it as decision DRN-3886351which can be viewed on the FOS' website.

outstanding Bounce Back Loan debt. The Ombudsman ordered that NatWest must allow the company to be dissolved and write off the Bounce Back Loan debt. Had this decision not found its way to the Ombudsman, then NatWest would have benefitted by placing the £2,000 debt in default, causing the debt to be indemnified by the British Business Bank.

On 22 March 2022, Will Dunn of The New Statesman[23] interviewed Graham Barrow of Transparency International[24] about failings in Companies House, in particular the issue of Bounce Back Loans being issued to companies that were dormant or had been quickly struck off the register after a loan had been granted. The article reported that 3,000 businesses a day are registered with Companies House, 10% of which are registered by Albanians who make up 0.5% of the population. It also reported that HMRC is not linked to the data held at Companies House and that it is easy for companies to be set up in your name without your knowledge. It is easy for money launderers to set up a company in the UK from anywhere in the world and then establish a bank account for that company, again from anywhere in the world. Money is washed through shell companies many times before it lands in offshore tax havens. The Economic Crime Act 2022 was designed to force the beneficial owners of companies to reveal their identities.

The data held by Companies House is often out of date or inaccurate. I had a conversation with Lucca De Paoli, at that time a journalist with Business Matters,[25] who was interested in writing an article of the Subject and wanted to speak to some of my clients. He mentioned that the day before he had attended a Court in London and witnessed Barclays[26] make 54 applications for insolvency in respect of defaulted or fraudulent Bounce Back Loan applications. On the same day I had been in a police station with a client who was suspected of making a fraudulent application for a Bounce Back Loan by Santander and was being interviewed under caution by the National Investigation Service (NATIS).[27] The striking similarity was this: in the court hearings reported to me by Lucca De Paoli, several directors had claimed to the judge that Barclays had got it wrong because Companies House records showing that their company was dormant were factually incorrect. My client was able to prove

23 See www.newstatesman.com/business/2022/03/why-kleptocrats-and-money-launderers-love-companies-house

24 Transparency International is a global organisation which aims to end the injustice of corruption; see transparencyschool.org/lecturer/graham-barrow/

25 www.bmmagazine.co.uk

26 Barclays refers to Barclays Bank PLC; see www.barclays.co.uk

27 The National Investigation Service investigates serious crime where public funds and the public authorities that manage them have been targeted. It works with UK law enforcement and government nationally. It has staff based across the UK. It is a service of Thurrock Council. www.thurrock.gov.uk/fraud-and-other-economic-crime/national-investigation-service-natis

that his company was not dormant, contrary to Companies House records and alleged by Santander, and avoided prosecution.

The NATIS investigator confided in me that banks placing Bounce Bank Loans into default and falsely alleging fraud was a massive issue. In his words 'It's another Post Office scandal'. The banks were passing the debt back to the BBB which was then under a duty to refer the cases to NATIS. When the NATIS investigated, it found no evidence of fraud. The banks were taking it as read that Companies House records were accurate and defaulting without any further investigation. It is obvious that many of the 'investigations' conducted by the banks were no more than cursory examinations of faulty public records.

This brings me onto David's case. He was happy to talk to the journalist and did so, but others felt uncomfortable about doing so. Out of respect for his privacy I have given him an alias.

HSBC had loaded a Cifas marker against David for making a fraudulent Bounce Back Loan application. He was self-employed at the time he made the application and in my view was permitted to apply. His self-employed business was new, had generated no income in 2018, and only started gathering momentum in 2019. He and his accountant believed that David could make a projection of earnings in respect of the Bounce Back Loan application, and in fact his earnings exceeded those expectations. HSBC relied on an innocuous note at the end of David's SA302[28] tax declaration as its reason for loading the marker. His accountant confirmed that he had left the note by mistake from a previous years' SA302, and HMRC confirmed that the note would have had no impact on the tax calculation, which was correct. Having refused to remove the marker, and after Cifas upheld the marker, we took the case to the FOS which found against HSBC which in turn agreed to remove the marker. Exceptionally the FOS also ordered HSBC to pay David's legal costs. The salient issue is this: bad decisions based on poor interpretation of data cause injustice. David had lost his business, his home and he had to sell his car because he could not get finance to insure it. He had done nothing wrong and was repaying the loan; he had not defaulted and wanted to pay the loan. I believe that there are many similar cases out there to David's.

Many issues with Bounce Back Loans are surfacing years after the loans were taken out. Once the loans are placed in default, usually because the company has folded or cannot afford to keep up the repayments, some banks will load Cifas markers against the directors. The reason for this is twofold. First, Cifas markers can be used when a debt is owed, not just when fraud is suspected, because the Subject presents a risk to the banking community which the system says needs to be warned of that risk. The second reason is, because borrowers were not asked to take personal guarantees under the BBLS;

28 SA302 tax declaration refers to the declaration someone completes when submitting their tax returns to HMRC.

there was no provision for it. Consequently, some banks are now ensuring that the directors do not avoid personal liability by loading Cifas markers against them. Usually when a personal guarantee is called in by a bank, a CCJ could be obtained if the guarantor fails to pay, which in turn could create credit worthiness issues for the guarantor for the next six years. CCJs can be removed once the liability has been cleared, but it remains to be seen whether the banks will agree to the removal of Cifas markers if debts are repaid in Bounce Back Loan cases.

As for the NATIS investigator's assertion that the Bounce Back Loan scandal was bigger than the Post Office Horizon scandal, I do not know how many individuals have been affected, but there are common denominators. The obvious one is that large private organisations can sometimes use their power and influence unreasonably and forcefully to recover money from subordinate 'little people', not caring about the adverse impact on their customers' businesses or reputations. As an example, consider the scandal involving utility companies being forced to climb down from forcing pre-payment meters on customers. But there are more commonalities than that, some of which are subtle and which are directly relevant to the Subject matter of this book and my question: is it right for the standard of proof for loading markers to be below that of criminal standard?

This is a timely moment to contrast the civil standard 'reasonable suspicion' level of investigation used by financial organisations to load fraud markers with the practices expected by the criminal justice system when prosecuting criminal offences in the courts.

The Post Office prosecutions were brought as Private Prosecutions. This is because the Post Office is a private company, not a department of state. The right to bring private prosecutions is enshrined in English and Welsh law. Lord Wilberforce stated in *Gouriet v Union of Post Office Workers (1978) 3 All ER 70 [1977]:*

> The individual, in such situations, who wishes to see the law enforced has a remedy of his own: he can bring a private prosecution. This historical right which goes right back to the earliest days of our legal system, though rarely exercised in relation to indictable offences . . . remains a valuable constitutional safeguard against inertia or partiality on the part of authority.

That right goes back to the 1700s. However, private prosecutions became less common when the Prosecution of Offences Act 1879 came into being. That act laid the foundations for a national police force to be created. The right was preserved by section 6(1) of the Prosecution of Offences Act 1985, the government legislation that gave the Crown Prosecution Service[29] the statutory

29 The Crown Prosecution Service is an independent body which prosecutes cases on behalf of the police and other government agencies; see www.cps.gov.uk

duty to take over the conduct of all criminal proceedings brought by the police (its duty can be found in Section 3(2) of that act). It is perhaps a combination of that legislation with the passing of the Data Protection Act 1988 that enabled Cifas to be established in 1988 and perhaps why its standard of proof was initially set to the criminal standard.

There are advantages to allowing organisations and individuals to privately prosecute cases, since they do not need to rely on the police to investigate. However, the courts have been increasingly mindful that private prosecution cases must reach state standard. The judgment delivered by Lord Justice Gross, in the case of *R (Kay and another) v Leeds Magistrates' Court (2018) 4 WLR 91* bringing an end to a private prosecution, quashing a decision of the Magistrates' Court, stated:

> Advocates and solicitors who have the conduct of private prosecutions must observe the highest standards of integrity, or regard for the public interest and duty to as a Minister for Justice in preference to the interests of the client who has instructed them to bring the prosecution; owing a duty to the court to ensure that the proceeding is fair.

In 2020, the Justice Select Committee,[30] concerned about the miscarriage of justice found during the Post Office Horizon scandal, questioned the effectiveness of existing safeguards and the merits of additional safeguards that could be used to limit the right to bring private prosecutions by large organisations. I provided written evidence supporting the right of large organisations to continue to bring private prosecutions.[31]

At the time I provided my evidence I was (and still am) a member of the Private Prosecutors' Association.[32] It had established a 'Code for Private Prosecutors' based on the Code for Crown Prosecutors[33] which is the standard used by the CPS when bringing prosecutions for the police and other state departments. I argued that, provided the Code for Private Prosecutors was followed and there was independent legal oversight of the prosecutions, then that should be sufficient safeguard to prevent miscarriage of justice.

30 The Justice Select Committee is a Parliamentary committee which examines various topical issues relating to the Criminal Justice System; see committees.parliament.uk/committee/102/justice-committee

31 A PDF of the arguments I put forward can be found at PPS0007 through this link. committees.parliament.uk/committee/102/justice-committee/publications/written-evidence/?page=26

32 The Private Prosecutors' Association is a private body which has established a voluntary code of conduct (the Code for Private Prosecutors) to guide those commencing private criminal prosecutions in England and Wales; see Home – Private Prosecutors . . .' Association (private-prosecutions.com)

33 The Code for Crown Prosecutors describes the standard that needs to be satisfied for the CPS to commence a prosecution. There is an ongoing duty to review a case against the Code (also known as the Full Code test); see private-prosecutions.com/ppa-code-foreword/

It is now clear that the Post Office had failed to follow the Code for Crown Prosecutors when deciding to prosecute cases. It used its prosecutions for entirely commercial purposes knowing that the evidence on which the prosecutions were based was flawed. It breached the Criminal Procedure and Investigation Act 1996 (CPIA),[34] principally ensuring that the investigations were fair and impartial, considering all reasonable lines of enquiry with an open mind to ensure that all avenues leading to and away from guilt were explored.[35] The Criminal Procedure Rules[36] set clear parameters that did not exist at the time the Post Office prosecutions were brought. To bring a private prosecution now, the court must consider fully the essential ingredients of the alleged offences, that there must be prima facie[37] evidence of an offence having been committed. The courts are now more aware that defendants can attack prosecutions where there has been an abuse of process and that the CPS can be asked to independently review a case and intervene and stop the case if it considers that the full code test has not been met or where there is a wider public interest for it to adopt and continue the prosecution.

In that sense there was a crossover with the previous standard of proof set out by Cifas. The aim was to ensure that the evidence was sufficiently rigorous that it presented a prima facie case that the police could investigate further if it so wished.

Many organisations bring private prosecutions for regulatory offences and have a statutory duty to prosecute. For example, water companies prosecute where offences contrary to the Water Industry Act 1981 have been committed and, ironically, given the outcry over the state of watercourses in the UK adversely impacted by raw sewage dumping, were they not to prosecute then they could themselves face sanction by the Environment Agency.

I wrote in my submissions:

> The fact the Post office Horizon cases have now been opened up for appeal following a rigorous examination by the Criminal Case Review Commission[38] is in itself fair warning to large organisations that private prosecutions must be fair and impartial.

34 The Criminal Procedure and Investigations Act 1996 established the rules which investigations into criminal conduct should follow; see www.gov.uk/government/publications/criminal-procedure-and-investigations-act-code-of-practice

35 Point 3.5 of the Code of Practice CPIA 1996 (Section 23.1)

36 The Criminal Procedure Rules 2020 SI no. 759 is the latest reincarnation of the rules that the courts follow throughout the course of criminal case, from first hearing to trial.

37 Prima facie, a Latin phrase used in criminal law that means 'at first sight'; see dictionary.cambridge.org/dictionary/english/prima-facie

38 The Criminal Case Review Commission is an independent body that considers whether convictions for serious offences such as murder are safe; see www.ccrc.gov.uk

I went on to say,

> I believe the risk of miscarriage of justice when bringing private prosecutions is now much reduced, particularly if the Code for Private Prosecutors is followed and experiences independent investigators and lawyers are instructed'. In conclusion I stated, 'I also hope that over the passage [of time] it will be seen that the miscarriage of justice caused by the Post Office Horizon cases was of its time and never repeated.

In its findings, the Justice Select Committee recommended that the government regulate the use of private prosecutions and limit the costs that could be awarded to those that the state (CPS) would claim, which were far lower than the rates claimed by private prosecutors.

My representations were written in June 2020, just as the first of my post-Covid fraud marker cases were coming through. I had no idea at that time that events surrounding Bounce Back Loans – or the inappropriate use of fraud markers – would make my rather trusting arguments to the Justice Select Committee appear somewhat misplaced.

At the time of writing this book, the public inquiry into the Post Office Horizon scandal is ongoing, and it has revealed many shocking examples of where public officials put the Post Office's interests before justice. Detailed commentary on the evidence considered by the ongoing inquiry is beyond the scope of this book, but I have found a few highlights to refer to. I also refer to Nick Wallis' book, *The Great Post Office Scandal*,[39] to discuss the correlation between the way in which the Post Office behaved and the way in which the banks have treated the BBLS and their customers and the way in which Cifas markers are loaded against innocent people who may be unable to prove their innocence through no fault of their own.

The first correlation is that the Subpostmasters had to prove that there was something wrong with the Horizon computer system; if they could not then they would be convicted, usually of False Accounting on an almost strict liability basis. The Post Office relied on the fact that, in the absence of evidence to the contrary, there are legal presumptions about technology working and being incapable of failure.[40] This was an almost impossible hurdle for the defendants to overcome, and many were advised or chose to plead guilty to

39 Bath Publishing ISBN 9781739 099206

40 Section 69 Police and Criminal Evidence Act 1984 (evidence from computer records inadmissible unless conditions relating to proper use and operation of computer shown to be satisfied) removed by Section 60 Youth Justice and Criminal Evidence Act 1999. The Police and Criminal Evidence Act 1984 Sets out the rules to be followed by the police and other organisations investigating, arresting, and detaining in custody those suspected of committing criminal offences; see www.legislation.gov.uk/ukpga/1984/60/contents

lesser offences to avoid the almost inevitable loss of credit following conviction after a trial they were almost certain to lose.

With Cifas and other fraud markers systems, the banks impose a reverse burden of proof on the Subject to prove their innocence before agreeing to remove markers. As David's case demonstrates, the banks nit-pick, and any discrepancy can be used to assume fraud has been committed. Some organisations rely solely on automated decision-making processes to assess the data they are provided with, such as in motor insurance and car finance applications, and if there are discrepancies will then load the applicants' details to a fraud database without further investigation. Some organisations refuse to remove markers even where the Subject can prove their innocence, and when they do so the alleged offending of the Subject is effectively turned into one of strict liability, akin to offences such as driving without insurance and regulatory offences. This compares unfavourably to the criminal law where intention and dishonesty[41] are essential elements of fraud that need to be established beyond reasonable doubt to convict.

This is particularly unfair for many who only realise several years down the line that they have been marked but due to the passage of time cannot find evidence to support their innocence. I have lost count of the number of people who have complained to me that they have lost their evidence over time, and if only they had known. . . . Such complaints are a daily occurrence, hence the scale of the injustice caused by these markers is potentially enormous. In maintaining the practice of not notifying customers about the imposition of Cifas and other fraud markers when money laundering is alleged, it is arguable that member organisations of the fraud databases are, like the Post Office, creating an inequality of arms that is grossly unfair to the genuinely innocent.

Many an injustice has been caused by this lack of transparency, which for legal reasons ('tipping off') is sometimes unavoidable (which I addressed in the previous chapter). For straightforward fraudulent application cases transparency is perfectly permissible and desirable. The banks' use of assumptions is widespread, developed through machine-learning, algorithms, and artificial intelligence. We know that NatWest invested £700 million in fraud prevention measures between 2019 and 2022.[42] The smaller banks, like the challengers Starling, Monzo, and Revolut, do not have such large budgets and therefore make more use of assumptions. One former bank investigator in a top five bank who came to me to help him to (successfully) remove a Cifas marker told me that investigators only had 20 minutes to make decisions on whether

41 The legal test for dishonesty is set out in *Ivey v. Genting Casinos (UK) Ltd t/a Crockfords (2017) UKSC 67*

42 www.thisismoney.co.uk/money/markets/article-10499989/Natwest-boss-Alison-Rose-pledges-1bn-fight-fraud-five-years.html

to load markers or not, and so even the big banks do not have the financial resources to investigate cases thoroughly.

Which brings me to the second issue, the similarities and failings in the way cases were/are investigated by the banks and Post Office Horizon scandal.

The Post Office used internal investigators reporting to in-house lawyers who made decisions on whether charges should be brought. There was an independent firm of Solicitors that was engaged by the Post Office to present cases in court, and whilst initially it appeared to have been kept in the dark about the reality of the failures in the Horizon system, evidence has come to light in the public inquiry that shows that may not be the case. It also became apparent that Post Office investigators ignored the concerns they had in relation to the Horizon system's integrity. The former senior tech lead at the Post Office, Jeremy Folkes, reportedly spoke to the Inquiry about 'confirmation bias', believing that the system was working correctly in providing data, and in response investigators and prosecutors did not question whether the data could be relied upon.[43] Another IT expert, Andrew Simpkins, told the Inquiry that he did not know that the Post Office investigations team existed or that people were being prosecuted. He questioned why during the development of the system it had not been identified that people could go to prison because of the data generated by the Horizon system. In his article for the *Empty City*,[44] Paul Marshall, a barrister who represented wrongly accused Subpostmasters, argued that legal and corporate contexts facilitated the wrongdoing behind the Post Office scandal. This occurred when individuals in organisations misconceived their roles and functions and in so doing incorrectly protected their employers' interests.[45] It is now known that the investigators employed by the Post Office received no training, as was admitted by one of the investigators, Gary Thomas, who also confirmed on oath to the Inquiry chaired by Sir Whyn Thomas that he had no prior experience of conducting criminal investigations. Neither did he understand the law of the offences he was tasked with investigating; theft and false accounting. He admitted to conducting Police and Criminal Evidence Act 1984 (PACE)[46] interviews without being trained into how to conduct interviews; transcripts demonstrated the use of closed questions and the use of baseless bias (that there was nothing wrong with the Horizon system). He also admitted to using identification codes which are no more than racial profiling which create bias against groups that become targeted unjustly for investigation.

43 www.computerweekly.com/news/252526883/Confirmation-bias-led-Post-Office-to-prosecute-subpostmasters-without-investigation-inquiry-told

44 The Empty City www.emptycity.substack.com

45 www.emptycity.substack.com/p/how-the-legal-system-made-it-so-easy?publication_id=474138&utm_campaign=email-post-title&r=ty5

46 Interviews held in accordance with Code E to the Police and Criminal Evidence Act 1984 www.gov.uk/government/publications/pace-codes-e-and-f-2018/pace-code-e-2018-accessible

And the correlation in the context of fraud markers? I have acted for several fraud investigators who have asked for my assistance to challenge fraud markers loaded against them, and in the course of taking instructions it became obvious that they were inadequately trained, poorly educated (several have had no qualifications or prior experience) and are being siloed by organisations, considering very specific issues that might lead to the conclusion that a fraud might be being committed without looking at the wider context. As for interviewing techniques? With very few notable exceptions, interviews are next to non-existent. Some banks use messaging systems and apps to conduct investigations; almost without exception they are perfunctory and do not follow lines of enquiry or ask follow-up questions to ascertain whether the Subject has a defence. There is little transparency and explanation about the consequences of failing to provide information; many Subjects are confused by the process. Assumptions are then made about guilt or innocence, and no regard is made for false negatives. I have even been asked on a couple of occasions by different fraud investigators to explain what the different types of Cifas markers mean. This level of ignorance sometimes applies to those considering applications for finance too. I am frequently contacted by people who have discovered that they have victim of impersonation markers loaded against them – which should not have an adverse impact on their ability to apply for credit – but who are having applications declined due to the existence of a 'Cifas marker'.

When I provided written evidence to The Justice Select Committee regarding proposed safeguards for private prosecutions, I argued that ideally a private prosecutor should instruct independent investigators and lawyers, mimicking the way in which the CPS and Police work. I wrote 'it is not always practical, desirable or possible for large organisations to instruct independent investigators, particularly where they wish to prosecute using statutory powers, for example through the Water Industry Act 1981, or byelaws'. Further:

> The specialist knowledge of staff working for such large organisations is a valuable resource when identifying such "regulatory" offences because they can use that understanding when they investigate cases. Some of which are lengthy and conducted during the course of their duties, noting and evidencing when breaches have occurred in order to build the case. They would not be suitable for independent investigators to intervene; in my experience properly trained specialist staff can produce excellent evidential files.

The problem I saw it was this:

> The situation regarding the Post Office Horizon prosecutions can be distinguished from the regulatory cases described above because the Post Office itself was the alleged victim and there were no wider issues as with

> the regulatory offences described. Whilst it is always in the public interest to prosecute fraud, the Post Office, as a limited company, was clearly conflicted when it instructed its own internal investigators to conduct the investigation. The criticisms are obvious; it was investigating its own staff but ignored flaws in its own systems.[47]

I have seen no evidence of independent or legal oversight regarding the decision to load markers; the internal investigators have the final call on whether to load markers. Previously, it was clear that the standard required the evidence to be sufficiently robust for it to be capable of being submitted to the police. Now, with that requirement deleted, how are the organisations to judge whether the evidence is sufficiently robust, particularly if their staff are unqualified and siloed into investigating salient aspects of fraud rather than considering the bigger picture?

Next, Nick Wallis demonstrated in his book that the Post Office obstructed the truth; his opinion has been confirmed in the evidence heard by the Inquiry. The Post Office was corrupted by a desire not to admit the truth; instead, it chose to hide its activities. It felt it was not in the public interest to disclose the failings with the Horizon system. Did that amount to dishonesty? As discussed earlier, dishonesty cannot be formed by a corporation, but the controlling minds, the individuals making decisions, can form the mens rea to become dishonest. I am not going to discuss the dishonest individuals who were highlighted by Nick Wallis and who have been criticised publicly having given evidence to the Inquiry; plenty has been written elsewhere on that Subject. But those senior lawyers in the Post Office, who are either Solicitors or Barristers and who are therefore professionally regulated, are Officers of the Supreme Court of England and Wales. They have a professional duty not to mislead the Court; that duty is intrinsic in their respective professions' codes of conduct. They are under investigation by the SRA. Barristers have a different set of 'Core Duties' which are set out by their governing body, the Bar Standards Board.[48]

Any in-house lawyer working for a financial organisation that is a member of one of the fraud databases needs to clearly appreciate and acknowledge the fact that their professional duty to act independently and honestly is non-negotiable, regardless of their role when acting for a corporate

47 A PDF of the arguments I put forward can be found at PPS0007 at www.committees.parliament.uk/committee/102/justice-committee/publications/written-evidence/?page=26

48 The Bar Standards Board, the governing and regulatory authority for the Barristers profession. A Barrister (otherwise known as 'Counsel') is a legal expert in evidence and advocacy, typically practising in the Higher Courts (High Court for civil and Crown Court for criminal) within their chosen fields of expertise. The highest tier of barristers become Kings Counsel (KC) and frequently – but not exclusively – become members of the judiciary; see www.barstandardsboard.org.uk/for-barristers/bsb-handbook-and-code-guidance/the-bsb-handbook.html

organisation either internally or externally. I have seen judgments from Courts where banks have told the Courts (via their lawyers) that applications for banking and finance are not dependent on whether fraud markers are loaded against the Subject. Theoretically that may be true, but that is not what I see in practice. The common denominator with all the thousands of people who have come to me for help me is that they have all been refused credit or banking facilities. The majority who have had multiple bank accounts have seen some of their other accounts close; many have no accounts left at all. Confirmation bias sets into customer onboarding decision making processes when fraud markers are flagged. There are very few organisations that will provide banking and credit facilities to those with fraud markers, and the limited number of products that are available tend to be less comprehensive or are more expensive. One wealthy client told me that the only new car he was able to obtain finance on was a Ferrari! I am not aware of any mainstream business or company accounts available to those with fraud markers recorded against them. Nor was my Ferrari-driving client. He had to run his successful business through his personal account and hoped his bank didn't spot what he was doing – which was in breach of his bank's terms and conditions – or the marker. In either scenario it would have resulted in his last remaining account being closed. Somehow, he managed to survive; many others have not.

Then we come to lack of regulatory oversight. Nick Wallis rightly criticised the lack of regulatory intervention in the Post Office. It has taken a public inquiry to uncover the truth at the most enormous expense to the public purse.

Regulatory oversight of the banks, through the FCA, could be improved. The rules are wieldy and cause unfairness to many consumers. Justice and fairness are not built into fraud marker systems, and some will feel have they been designed for the benefit of the banks without regard to anyone else.

As with the Post Office, some banks choose not to admit mistakes. I have a naughty list. There are some banks that are fairer than others.

There is also a comparison in the way in which organisations are more concerned with self-serving interests rather than using lawful means. The Post Office used criminal prosecutions to recover money, in violation of the full code test of the Code of Crown Prosecutors. Had it been known what the Post Office's true policy was at the time it brought proceedings, then the Subpostmasters would have had grounds to argue that the prosecutions were malicious, could have asked the CPS to intervene, and then would have been entitled to damages had the CPS adopted and then withdrawn their case. Ironically it is now known that the CPS prosecuted several Horizon cases for the Post Office. It is truly scandalous that so many Subpostmasters have not yet been compensated. It is extremely rare for compensation to be offered or awarded to recipients of incorrectly loaded fraud markers, and even then, the sums are paltry. As mentioned previously, allegedly some banks encouraged customers to take out Bounce Back Loans, only to find nefarious reasons to default on those same loans, loading markers which ruined lives as a result. Not for the first time have banks miss-sold products, as the PPI scandal demonstrates.[49]

Many Subpostmasters did not have the stomach for a fight. I see similarities with fraud marker cases; many potential clients choose not to fight, generally because they don't have the headspace or the pocket for it. As with the behaviour of kleptocrats, the Post Office used strong-arm tactics to scare off civil claims. The technical term for such behaviour is Strategic Litigation Against Public Participation (SLAPP) which the Government and SRA are concerned about stamping out.[50] Financial organisations need to appreciate that most people will be frightened of the costs consequences of taking them to court. Thankfully, there are cost effective routes of arbitration available to challenge fraud markers, but, as explained previously, the rules mean too many cases fall through the gaps leaving little choice for Subjects other than expensive litigation if the organisations cannot be persuaded to voluntarily remove markers.

Next, we come to lack of disclosure. The Post Office refused to provide information when requested that would have undermined the prosecution or assisted the defence; the test that applies is in the disclosure rules set out in the Criminal Procedure and Investigations Act 1996 (CPIA) and there is no doubt that those rules were breached. In a similar vein, some banks are more obstructive than others when Data Subject Access Requests (DSAR) are made rather than entering the spirit of the request to ascertain whether an injustice has been created.

Cifas is more transparent in the way it operates than National Hunter and Synectic Solutions, but all need to do more. Cifas' refusal to allow lawyers access to its rule book is uncomfortable, placing Subjects at a disadvantage. Isn't lack of transparency obstructing the truth? After all, if a suspect in a police station is interviewed and answers no comment to all questions asked, an adverse inference can be drawn by the court regarding that refusal to co-operate, including that the suspect was dishonest about not being transparent with the truth. Isn't the reverse the case with banks such as Santander that take an overly legalistic approach when refusing to co-operate with DSARs? After all, mistakes frequently happen such as when NatWest admitted it had made an 'administrative error' when de-banking Yad Vashem UK.[51] Why shouldn't

49 See www.which.co.uk/news/article/ppi-mis-selling-scandal-an-insider-view-aN85r6g9Pm6i

50 Strategic Litigation Against Public Participation is the practice of using the threat of inappropriate litigation in civil cases to warn off or prevent a party to proceedings from proceeding further; see www.gov.uk/government/consultations/strategic-lawsuits-against-public-participation-slapps/outcome/strategic-lawsuits-against-public-participation-slapps-government-response-to-call-for-evidence

51 See www.dailymail.co.uk/news/article-13774655/Fury-NatWest-debanks-one-Britains-biggest-Holocaust-memorials-no-explanation.html

the innocent victim of a mistake not be allowed every opportunity to right a wrong against them? There is nothing to prevent banks from providing redacted data, as many do. Cifas will now provide copies of documents considered to have been altered and submitted with applications, but in identity theft cases it is vital that the innocent Subject is provided with as much information as possible to help them to prove their innocence.

The final point of this analogy is racism. Although he could not provide data to prove his theory, Nick Wallis believed that there was a racist element when looking at the number of racial minority background Subpostmasters who were prosecuted. I cannot verify my figures either, but I also see trends, and most of my clients are from racial minorities.

Banks are not good at learning lessons from past mistakes. I refer to the HBOS banking scandal. Halifax Bank of Scotland (HBOS), which is now part of Lloyds Banking Group PLC (Lloyds),[52] was accused of knowing about the wrongdoing of three of its managers and that it failed to investigate properly. A six-year-long investigation by Thames Valley Police revealed that between 2003 and 2007 HBOS' employees Lyden Scourfield and David Mills – who worked in the HBOS Impaired Assets Division – and others unconnected with HBOS had conspired to corrupt and engage in fraudulent trading and a conspiracy to conceal criminal property. The crimes committed resulted in Lloyds compensating the victims to the tune of £600 million. Scourfield and Mills were convicted in January 2017. Lloyds, which took over HBOS after the allegations came to light, publicly apologised for the harm done to victims.[53] It also recognised that the compensation scheme it established in the wake of the convictions, whilst 'generous and in excess of what would have been awarded by a court', did not deliver 'fair and reasonable outcomes for all customers'. It has offered to re-review the cases in question. The All-Party Parliamentary Group on Fair Business Banking considered the issues raised during its investigation and subsequently reported that Lloyds has accepted that there was 'cultural tendency' to adopt 'an overly defensive and legalistic approach to external challenges rather than taking time to engage with complainants to understand their perspective in full'. The report found that Lloyd's approach to the victims of the fraud 'lacked understanding and empathy' which 'created unnecessary confrontation'.[54]

Why then do so many banks continue to take an overly legalistic approach to considering whether fraud markers should be removed? Are they frightened to confront the injustice caused to the victims of fraud? Are banks

52 Lloyds Banking Group trades under numerous brands; see www.lloydsbankinggroup.com

53 See www.lloydsbankinggroup.com/investors/shareholder-information/hbos-reading-update-on-historic-failures.html

54 hansard.parliament.uk/Commons/2018-10-09/debates/362E54F9-B141-45B9-8029-D8AA14144453/BusinessBankingFraud

more concerned with protecting their reputations than admitting to mistakes and hardship caused to customers? The comparison with the behaviour of the Post Office is stark. In my opinion the lessons learned by Lloyds dealing with the HBOS scandal have generally not been learnt by the wider banking community. When challenging markers for clients I have experienced lack of empathy, lack of understanding, lack of humanity, and organisations being unnecessarily confrontational and legalistic. Some are plain rude, refusing to respond to complaints or failing to provide final response letters confirming that markers have been removed; several clients have only discovered they have won their case when they carry out fresh checks of the databases. In 2024 the All-Party Parliamentary Group on Fair Business Banking formed the view that if de-banking were to occur unfairly and not proportionately, then it would act.[55]

Which leads to the next question; how will fraud markers develop? How will governments, banks, and regulators in other countries respond, and will they build better and fairer systems?

55 www.standard.co.uk/news/politics/banks-mps-financial-conduct-authority-government-parliament-b1140598.html

4 The international reach of fraud databases

The fraud marker systems are developing, utilising new technology and a greater understanding of the criminal mindset to predict whether Subjects pose a threat to the banking and finance community and, by translation, to society. The threats posed by money launderers, organised crime networks, kleptocrats and terrorist financing is international. Cifas is seen as the benchmark by countries seeking to combat such threats, especially in those seeking to embrace Faster Payments systems.

Faster Payments systems have caused well-publicised problems elsewhere in the world, notably Australia. It was an issue the House of Lords was alive to when recommending that the banks should be able to delay larger transactions or those to new payees to allow banks the time to investigate and contact consumers about proposed payments. It explained that new technology, such as Faster Payments and Open Banking,[1] allow transactions to be made with greater speed; in the case of Faster Payments transactions take place almost instantly. The report mentioned that, in 2021, 3.4 billion transactions were processed through this system. Open Banking allows the sharing of transaction data more easily. But Faster Payments were used in 96% of APP frauds, an increase of 34% on the year before, albeit that APP fraud accounted for 0.0066% of payments made through this system. The use of Confirmation of Payee questions during the transaction processing is causing fraudsters to target victims whose banks do not use this system. In July 2023 the FCA's New Consumer Duty[2] came into force, which followed the House of Lords report by proposing that banks should consider building 'positive friction' into processes. Increased data sharing between payments firms is also proposed. As I understand it, these proposals will take at least a couple of years

1 Open banking allows for the sharing of banking data with organisations, such as government or credit providers; see www.moneysavingexpert.com/banking/open-banking/

2 The FCA's new Consumer Duty establishes outcomes for customers that relate to products and services; price and value; consumer understanding; and consumer support. www.fca.org.uk/publications/policy-statements/ps22-9-new-consumer-duty

DOI: 10.4324/9781003588542-4

to be enabled. But the increased risk of fraud created by the Faster Payments systems is obvious, and countries that embrace it need to meet those threats.

How countries counter these threats is a complicated issue because each country has different policies, laws, and capabilities. Fraud and money laundering takes place on an international scale, sometimes with participants operating in different countries, and as the prosecution of the Black Axe gang in Ireland demonstrates, the use of money mules is an integral part to that.[3] Other difficulties include how to share data between states and, at a local level, how to share data among private organisations, local law enforcement, and the state.

Cifas is certified to ISO/IEC 27001:2013, the international standard for operating an information security management system. Data transfer between states is increasing; the UK GDPR[4] provides existing data adequacy arrangements with the EU. In 2021 the UK signalled post-Brexit global data sharing partnerships with the US (commercial organisations), Australia, Singapore, the Dubai International Finance Centre, and the Republic of Korea, indicating future partnerships with Kenya, Brazil, and India to build on existing data adequacy arrangements with New Zealand, Japan, Canada (commercial organisations), and the Crown Dependencies of Jersey, Guernsey, and the Isle of Man. Other countries that have GDPR like data provisions but which do not provide adequacy are China, Russia, Chile, Egypt, Nigeria, South Africa, Thailand, and Turkey.[5] The government press release stated that international data transfers are important for online banking among other reasons.[6] Other countries now recognised by the EU as having data adequacy are Andorra, Argentina, Israel, Switzerland, and Uruguay. Clearly there is still a long way to go before all nations are working to similar adequacy arrangements.

Researching international counter-fraud data sharing systems has been time consuming and difficult because many articles are hidden behind subscription paywalls. What has become apparent is that globally countries are moving at different speeds; some are glacial by comparison to others, but from what I have read the UK is setting the pace. The reason for that is necessity and an agile regulatory framework.

3 See www.sundayworld.com/crime/irish-crime/faces-of-black-axe-international-fraud-gang-members-after-being-busted-in-ireland/a357806436.html

4 The General Data Protection Regulation is an international standard of data compliance, with countries striving to work towards systems that, if not replicating each other entirely, provide adequacy for the safe transfer and storage of data. The Data Protection Act 2018, together with the UK General Data Protection Regulation (UK GDPR), establish and describe the UK's data protection regime; see www.ico.org.uk/for-organisations/uk-gdpr-guidance-and-resources/artificial-intelligence/guidance-on-ai-and-data-protection/about-this-guidance/?q=risk

5 See www.incountry.com/blog/data-residency-laws-by-country-overview/

6 See www.gov.uk/government/news/uk-unveils-post-brexit-global-data-plans-to-boost-growth-increase-trade-and-improve-healthcare

Necessity was driven by the butler enabling mindset of the financial service industry, Faster Payments systems, and a political elite that have attracted money launderers to the UK in droves. Swathing cuts to the finances of the criminal justice system and policing doubtless attracted hordes of international fraud actors to the UK and encouraged the domestic criminal fraternity to enable them. In short, the UK was forced to design fraud detection and data sharing facilities at pace; the speed of change has been enabled by a political culture that allows for independent private prosecutions and light touch regulation.

The rapid pace at which data sharing has been enabled in the UK is due in part to the Digital Economy Act 2017 which allowed for inter-government department data sharing agreements, known as the Public Service Delivery (PSD) power, to be made without the need for legislation by using statutory instruments to enable regulations. A relevant example is the Digital Government (Disclosure of Information, Identity Verification) Regulations 2023[7] which provides for one ID gateway into various government departments, creating a digital identity system without the need for ID cards and which protects 'the privacy of users and reduces identity fraud and theft'.

The Data Protection and Digital Information Bill[8] was the proposed legislation to replace the Data Protection Act 2018 which enabled UK GDPR equivalence with the EU GDPR. The Conservative UK Government was seeking through the Bill to 'enable the use of trusted digital identities' which extends to 'commercial products and services online'. However, passage of that legislation came to a halt in May 2024 when a general election was called, and it remains to be seen whether or when it will pass into law after the general election and, if it does, will it be revised?

Trust between state and private organisations has grown in the UK, creating a positive culture of co-operation. This is recognised in the Cross Government Fraud Functional Strategy 2024–2027;[9] it talks about using 'innovative technology and AI' and 'working closely with partners in the private sector to drive positive collaboration change' and supporting 'the government's continued professionalism of the counter fraud response'.

Previously the conservative government set out in the Economic Crime Plan 2, 2023 to 2026, proposals for reducing money laundering and combatting kleptocracy, cutting fraud, and reducing the threat of international illicit finance. It advocated even closer public private partnerships with a multi-agency approach through a public-private Economic Crime Data

7 www.legislation.gov.uk/ukdsi/2023/9780348251661

8 www.bills.parliament.uk/bills/3430

9 www.gov.uk/government/publications/government-counter-fraud-functional-strategy-2024-2027/cross-government-counter-fraud-functional-strategy-2024-2027-html

Strategy to 'enhance the exploitation of available data across the ecosystem to better prevent, detect, and pursue economic crime'.[10]

The UK counter-fraud community is highly motivated, well-funded, and innovative. For example, recently Pay UK, which operates Faster Payments, BACS[11] and direct debit has been working on a new fraud detection and prevention pilot with partners including Visa and Synectics Solutions using predictive technology 'detecting fraudulent activity before it occurs' with apparently excellent and eye opening results designed to prevent scams.[12] In July 2024 it was revealed that seven banks were working closely with the NCA to identify organised crime networks, sharing data and expertise.[13]

However, concerns are raised with me from time to time by professionals within the counter-fraud profession that not all organisations see the need to continue funding their roles when incidences of fraud are reduced; history shows that short sighted, profit driven attitudes lead to long-term disaster. Banks are accountable to their shareholders, but continued investment in counter-fraud should be removed from the grasp of bean counters because criminals are so far ahead of law enforcement and data protection systems; technology and infrastructure that proves itself safe one day can been proven utterly compromised the next. Organisations need look no further than the massive ransomware attack suffered by Citrix in 2023 as a clear warning of that.[14]

International organisations such as the FATF have placed countries under scrutiny regardless of loopholes, local levels of political corruption, and the turning of a blind eye to criminal activities; the threat to countries of being placed on the FATF black or grey list is not a badge many wish to tolerate for long. The latest to join the grey list of shame is one of the favourite homes for super rich tax dodgers, Monaco,[15] which in June 2024 suffered the indignity and embarrassment of increased monitoring designed to 'address strategic deficiencies in their regimes to counter money laundering, terrorist financing and proliferation financing'. Being placed on the grey list also means that regulated firms must undertake enhanced due diligence and ongoing monitoring of customers from such higher-risk jurisdictions. More than 200 countries now recognise the FATF; its recommendations are considered

10 www.gov.uk/government/publications/economic-crime-plan-2023-to-2026

11 See www.bacs.co.uk

12 www.wearepay.uk/pay-uks-fraud-detection-pilot-exceeds-expectations-detecting-over-112m-worth-of-fraud/

13 www.reuters.com/business/finance/seven-banks-share-data-with-uk-law-enforcement-dirty-money-crackdown-2024-07-26/

14 Citrix is an IT service provider which was infamously hacked causing massive disruption globally www.computerweekly.com/news/366560675/CISA-reveals-how-LockBit-hacked-Boeing-via-Citrix-Bleed

15 www.fatf-gafi.org/en/countries/black-and-grey-lists.html

the international standard for AML. Slowly but surely standards in banking practices and regulation are becoming homogenised, but the speed of travel is dependent on the adoption of data adequacy arrangements, and although there is a desire for harmonisation, in practice that is a slow process. *In Country* has produced a report setting out which countries it expects to announce data residency laws in 2024.[16]

The sharing of data between banks and government is haphazard across the world. Much depends on individual states' data sharing arrangements and agreements. GDPR creates friction in the sharing of data between organisations, and it is clear from my research that many countries feel hampered by legislation, which is time consuming to amend. Even within the EU, Cifas type organisations do not now exist. I found a similar system to Cifas in the Netherlands[17] that has been operating since 2021, TMNL,[18] but it has ceased operations prior to new Europe-wide AML legislation coming into force in 2027. For many years in Ireland there have been calls for a Cifas type organisation to be created, but until proposed changes to legislation there are implemented in 2024 it will not be able to become operational.[19]

In 2012 Professor Nicholas Ryder published *Money Laundering – An Endless Cycle: a comparative analysis of the anti-money laundering policies in the United States of America, the United Kingdom, Australia and Canada.*[20] Taking a retrospective look at how those policies have fared since 2012 provides an excellent opportunity to comment on the way in which the fraud databases systems have been developed, particularly in the UK, Australia and US. Canada still appears to be behind the curve, as explained further later.

The US seems to have moved forward considerably from the original National Money Laundering Strategy, which sought better links between law enforcement and financial institutions. The latest version of the US National Money Laundering Strategy which Ryder was able to comment on in his 2012 publication was the 2007 version.

The *2024 National Strategy for Combatting Terrorist and Other Illicit Financing*[21] ('2024 National Strategy') has built substantially on that early work. The four priorities the 2024 National Strategy concentrates on are to: assess and redress legal and regulatory gaps in the US AML/CFT regime; make the regulatory framework for financial institutions more risk focused and effective; enhance the operational effectiveness of law enforcement, which includes expanding and enhancing public-private information sharing (Action 10);

16 www.incountry.com/blog/data-residency-in-2024-laws-trends-and-insights
17 www.dataguidance.com/news/netherlands-ap-grants-licence-financial-institutions
18 www.tmnl.nl/en/
19 www.irishtimes.com/business/2024/02/07/industry-group-seeks-update-on-timeline-for-shared-fraud-database
20 Routledge ISBN 978-0-203-12678-3 (e-book)
21 www.home.treasury.gov/system/files/136/2024-Illicit-Finance-Strategy.pdf

and support responsible technological innovation and harness technology to mitigate illicit finance risks. There is no specific mention of fraud database participation, but it can be implied that it is part of US AML strategy as part of 'other relevant private sector entities' mentioned in Action 10, in particular 'Forging public-private partnerships through these sorts of factors provides a model to identify and disrupt a range of financial crimes'.[22] The 2024 National Strategy at page 22 also advocates whistle blowing for reward.

The Financial Crimes Enforcement Network (FinCEN)[23] is a public-private information sharing partnership of law enforcement and financial organisations in the US and is a key component of the 2024 National Strategy. Its stated aim is to combat money laundering to protect US citizens through a private-public partnership. FinCEN administers the Bank Secrecy Act 1970; suspicious financial transactions are reported to it which it shares with law enforcement, in a similar way to NCA's Financial Intelligence Unit (FIU) in the UK, the Australian Transaction Reports and Analysis Centre (AUSTRAC), and the Financial Transactions and Reports Analysis Centre of Canada.

The US and EU have established a Data Privacy Framework which includes an independent Data Protection Review Court to process EU citizens' complaints regarding the activities of US intelligence gathering which is limited to what is 'necessary and proportionate'. The 2024 National Strategy states that in 2023 some exchange events were convened by FinCEN to which it invited private organisations, although its website does not divulge which.

In the US the sharing of data is operated at a state by state rather than Federal level. It has two national level data sharing organisations that operate in a similar way to Cifas but without such a wide-ranging remit, although it is likely that they load fraud markers. Early Warning[24] is the most closely aligned to Cifas and provides data checking intelligence to approximately 2,500 financial organisations, retaining that data for five years. Early Warning operates the National Shared Database, Verify Account, Verify Deposit, and Predict New Account Risk systems which check personal information against authorised account owners.[25]

The other system I found reference to in the US is ChexSystems. It provides risk analysis of customers' previous financial behaviour[26] and holds data for 5 years. Poor credit ratings and risk are flagged to its business customers, making it more difficult for Subjects to obtain mainstream financial services. It claims these systems accord with the federal Fair Credit Reporting Act (FCRA). Its system, OnAlert, provides consumer monitoring of data

22 Page 29 2024 National Strategy
23 www.fincen.gov/resources/financial-crime-enforcement-network-exchange
24 www.earlywarning.com
25 www.earlywarning.com/sites/default/files/2023-07/Consortium_Data%20Sharing_A%20Valuable_Tool_in%20Fighting_Fraud.pdf
26 www.forbes.com/advisor/banking/chexsystems-everything-you-need-to-know

theft to its customers. It also operates to the federal Gamm-Leach-Bliley Act (GLBA), and operates several data analytics, data verification, and fraud detections systems. It provides disclosure reports to consumers on request.

FinCEN's Exchange is likely to contain many organisations other than Early Warning and ChexSystems. The 2024 National Strategy also referred to 'the Cross-Border Financial Crime Center' (CBFCC) which is another public-private partnership to enhance the US anti-money laundering strategy and includes federal law enforcement agencies, banks and financial institutions, financial technology companies, and 'partner nation authorities'. It also referred to the Five Eyes Law Enforcement Group (FELEG), a collaboration of law enforcement agencies in the United Kingdom, Australia, Canada, New Zealand, and the United States.

The Fair Credit Reporting Act 2023 allows data Subjects in the US to access data held by fraud databases for free once every 12 months. It also imposes a federal duty on organisations to investigate when Subjects dispute information and to notify Subjects when the reports are used to make adverse decisions that impact them.[27] The full report makes for an interesting comparison with the systems and laws described previously relating to the UK under the Data Protection Act 2018, ICO guidance, and UK GDPR. Highlights include the following:

Part 606(f) which defines the term 'consumer reporting agency' (duplicated and expanded at Part 606(p)) imposes a duty at Part 606 (r) (C) (i) to provide on request within five working days 'the nature and substance of all information in the consumer's file at the time of their request'. In the UK organisations are supposed to respond to DSARs within 30 days.

Part 606 (q)(2)(A) 'notifies all prospective users of a consumer report relating to the consumer that the consumer may be the victim of fraud'. Note that no such duty exists in the UK.

Part 606(u)(2) defines a 'reseller' as a consumer reporting agency that 'does not maintain a database of the assembled or merged information from which new consumer reports are produced'.

Part 604 defines 'Permissible purposes of consumer reports' which include among others those relating to credit, insurance, insolvency, army personnel and veterans and employment.

Part 605 (f) states that if a consumer disputes information furnished to the agency, then that fact shall be indicated in each consumer report. There is no equivalent provision in the UK.

Part 605A relates to fraud alerts relating to victims of fraud. Similar provision exists in the UK for the loading of victim of identify fraud markers, but in the UK there is no provision to notify the consumer. Many victims report

27 www.ftc.gov/legal-library/browse/statutes/fair-credit-reporting-act

back to me that the first they know of an issue is when accounts are blocked or applications for credit are denied; it is only when they consider their credit files that they may be able to see they have been marked to Cifas as a victim of identity theft, but some are not and are incorrectly marked with full fraud markers instead, the organisations failing to recognise that they are in fact victims. Garba, Lazarus, and Button discovered in their work referred to earlier that the US was targeted in 50% of the convictions of Nigerian crypto scammers; it stands to reason that the US fraud databases are going to include their victims.

The US 2024 National Strategy supports the US's relationship with the FATF which it recognises as having had a positive impact through the implementation of standards internationally, guiding countries to utilise and develop systems to disrupt criminal activity and prevent money laundering. It appears that international harmonisation of banking and funds transfers are on the horizon, with the FATF encouraging counties to adopt the ISO 20022 financial messaging standard following Swift's 'same activity, same risk, same rules' principles.[28]

I have not found reference to free-to-use arbitration systems in the US; unless organisations voluntarily remove markers the only way forward for Subjects is to commence likely expensive court proceedings.

According to Ryder, Canada was previously considered a concern as a major hub of money laundering due to its long border with the US and reliance on electronic banking. The Canadian Anti-Fraud Centre appears to operate a similar system to Action Fraud in the UK; collating information on fraud and scam alerts which it shares with the police. Open Banking regulation is proposed along similar lines to that available in the EU, UK, and Australia. Strong privacy protection laws in Canada prevent much private to private and private to public data sharing regarding potential illicit finance, although it is a partner in FELEG.

As Ryder noted, Australia was historically criticised by FATF. It became a hub for money laundering in the late 1980s and early 1990s, Ryder reporting that in 1989 $1.8 billion was laundered, yet by 1995 that had increased to $4.5 billion, with some reports indicating that figure had increased to $11.5 billion.[29] The FATF was concerned that the financial services sector in Australia was being targeted by money launderers. In response Australia adopted a range of international initiatives[30] including the Mutual Assistance in Criminal Matters (Money Laundering) Regulations 1997. As with the UK, Australia has been able to use regulations rather than primary legislation, a point discussed earlier in this chapter, a by-product of Australia's colonial past as part of the former British Empire.

28 www.iso20022.org
29 Page 104 Ryder
30 Page 106 Ryder

The FATF's 2024 4th Enhanced Follow-up Report[31] into measures taken by Australia shows progress has been made to address previously highlighted deficiencies in 2015. It reported that AUSTRAC[32] is moving towards developing a national fraud strategy. The Privacy Act 1988 places a requirement on businesses to comply with AML legislation. AUSTRAC regulates the 'access, use and disclosure of AML/CFT information' and consults with the Australian Information Commissioner regarding privacy, much the same as Cifas reports to the ICO and FCA in the UK.

The Australian Banking Association[33] collects and shares data in very limited circumstances. It is a member of the International Banking Federation (IBFed);[34] the UK is not. The Australian Financial Crimes Exchange[35] follows the work of Cifas and operates a marker system. It manages the Fraud Reporting Exchange (FRX) to report fraudulent (including scam) transactions 'between issuing and recipient financial institutions'. Its members are Australia and New Zealand Banking Group Limited, Commonwealth Bank of Australia, National Australia Bank Limited, and Westpac Banking Corporation. It has a recoveries process and offers one system for reporting. A Faster Payments type system called the New Payments Platform was introduced in February 2018. In 2021 the Australian Competition and Consumer Commission (ACCC) reported that $324 million had been notified to its reporting centre, Scamwatch, up 84% since 2019.

New Zealand's inclusion in FELEG is no surprise. It has data adequacy to the UK and requires banks to 'balance the public interest with respecting a customer's right to privacy' when it considers reporting suspicious transactions to the police.[36] It has a Banking Ombudsman Scheme to deal with complaints and, equivalent to the UK, an Office of the Privacy Commissioner. The FATF last assessed New Zealand in 2021,[37] reporting it to be delivering good results with a 'robust' and 'effective' AML/CFT system. However, I can find no reference to Cifas-like databases.

Other comparative systems to Cifas clearly do exist internationally but finding them has been a hit and miss exercise because the Cifas system does not appear to have been replicated fully, and if and where systems exist, they are frequently shrouded in secrecy. The FATF's reports do not mention specific systems; Cifas does not get a mention in its reports on the UK. Away from FELEG members, the nearest equivalent to a Cifas type system I could find was The South African Fraud Prevention Service.[38] It provides and maintains

31 www.fatf-gafi.org/en/publications/Mutualevaluations/Australia-fur-2024.html
32 www.austrac.gov.au
33 www.ausbanking.org.au/privacy-policy
34 www.ibfed.org.uk/about/members
35 www.afcx.com.au/afcx-exchange
36 www.bankomb.org.nz/guides-and-cases/quick-guides/other/privacy-and-confidentiality
37 www.fatf-gafi.org/en/publications/Mutualevaluations/Mer-new-zealand-2021.html
38 www.safps.org.za/Home/About

a fraud database which is affiliated to Cifas and offers a protective registration system. I am aware that South Africa has a similar insurance fraud database to the UK's IFR, as do Hong Kong, Canada, the US, Australia, Singapore, Korea, and China,[39] indicating that those non-FELEG member countries in this short list are likely to have similar systems available for banking and finance. However, such advanced systems have yet to help South Africa pull itself out of the FATF's grey list.

The only other countries with systems that are affiliated to Cifas are the Jersey Financial Intelligence Unit and the Gibraltar Financial Intelligence Unit.

In India, as recently as 2022 the banks sent information requests to the Central Economic Intelligence Bureau (CEIB) in physical form[40] causing delays to lending applications. That outdated practice sits uneasily beside its UPI faster payments system.[41] The Digital Personal Data Protection Bill is aimed at providing data adequacy with other states and is due to come into law in 2024. From that, as happened in New Zealand and is happening in Singapore,[42] data sharing between private organisations and the state is likely to flow more easily making it easier to disrupt scammers.

Rather than relying on individual states to support the creation of fraud databases such as Cifas, large international financial institutions could look to use borderless fraud detection systems such as Salv Bridge,[43] which is GDPR compliant across the EU and UK. Many of the tools mentioned in Chapter 1 are cross border, such as Swift.[44]

There are risks with international data transfer and countries operating on different rules and etiquette. Let's not forget that the banks have a problem with data security themselves. Consider this example from the US: in May 2023 HSBC was fined $45 million by the SEC for 'widespread and longstanding failures' by the firm and employees to 'maintain and preserve electronic communications'.[45] The regulator was concerned that employees were communicating on business matters through WhatsApp. Such practices were not confined to HSBC; Bank of America, Barclays, Credit Suisse,

39 www.international-adviser.com/hong-kong-urgently-launches-insurance-fraud-prevention-database

40 www.financialexpress.com/business/banking-finance-checking-frauds-pushing-big-ticket-spending-banks-seek-time-bound-data-sharing-from-ceib-2638822

41 www-bbc-com.cdn.ampproject.org/c/s/www.bbc.com/news/articles/c288m1km01po.amp

42 www.straitstimes.com/singapore/courts-crime/asset-recovery-a-priority-in-singapore-s-anti-money-laundering-regime-pm-wong

43 www.salv.com/blog/cifas-alternatives-competitors

44 www.swift.com/our-solutions/swift-gpi/stop-and-recall

45 www.fnlondon.com/articles/hsbc-fined-15m-for-whatsapp-monitoring-failures-20230511#:~:text=HSBC%20has%20been%20fined%20%2445,on%20messaging%20platforms%20like%20WhatsApp.

Deutsche Bank, Goldman Sachs, JP Morgan, Morgan Stanley, Nomura, Jefferies, and UBS were fined too, $2 billion all told. The use of social media in such circumstances presents a massive security and money laundering risk. In February 2023 it was reported that a data breach involving WhatsApp has enabled the details of nearly 500 million users to be purchased.[46] There have been other large-scale compromises of WhatsApp's data over past few years.

Since fraud and money laundering are international issues and the language used in counter-fraud is universal, it stands to reason that, unless banks continue to invest in new technology to keep pace with the latest threats and criminal intelligence, they will expose themselves to risk. Banks are using a suite of technologies to highlight risk, whether that is at an onboarding or transactional stage; the more tools they use the greater the chance they will be able to highlight fraudulent actors. The fraud databases referred to in this book are part of a bigger picture. In an article for Fintech Futures, Ouliana Smith argued that a solution to the problems is to design in fraud prevention solutions to digital banking platforms and that those that can deliver good consumer satisfaction whilst preventing fraud successfully will expand and thrive commercially.[47]

How data Subjects access the information held against them is a concern globally. GDPR helps to create a degree of conformity for data retention, but within that framework national policies differ.

The larger economies that have embraced faster payments systems have inadvertently increased their exposure to risk to fraud. But, if through greater transparency, education and greater use of technology they force organised crime networks to move money away from their jurisdictions, then to an extent it is arguable that the risk is transferred to less developed nations. Once money is transferred internationally, it becomes easier to detect. I suspect criminals will use ever more sophisticated techniques to ensure that they are not forced into the open. To that extent technology and data sharing will become ever more important in the fight against fraud and money laundering, but there is a trade-off in relation to data privacy and the risks exposed to data Subjects that needs more careful thought to prevent widespread injustice being caused.

46 See www.cybernews.com/news/whatsapp-data-leak

47 www.fintechfutures.com/2023/03/should-digital-banking-platforms-be-fraud-prevention-solutions-by-design

5 Justice and transparency – a fair balance?

I want to bring this book to a close by further considering the questions I outlined in Chapter 1.

Would greater transparency mean that many financial offences will be prevented from happening in the first place?

The banking and finance industry will point to the fact that joined up thinking and collaboration is starting to pay dividends. In June 2024, in a speech delivered by Steve Smart, the FCA explained to the Financial Services Investigations and Enforcement Summit that the 16% reduction in reported fraud incidents in 2023 compared to 2022 – and half a million fewer victims of fraud in that same time frame – was much to do with the multi-agency approach to tacking fraud and money laundering.[1] Key to that 'prevent' strategy is awareness, as he and so many others in the counter-fraud space have been exponents of for many years.

I have never understood why the organisations that load fraud markers have not explained in clearer terms to their customers about the fraud marker systems they use. Most of the people I have spoken to who have been affected by fraud markers have complained that they had no idea what Cifas is, including many working in banking and finance. If the banking and finance industries are so concerned about fighting fraud, why were they not open with their customers about the consequences of certain actions? All their terms and conditions will have contained phrases such as 'if you do not keep up repayments your home may be repossessed' or give warnings about contacting fraud protection agencies, but there is no black and white guidance anywhere about the consequences of actions other than to remark 'it may affect your ability to get credit'. As this book has explained, the consequences can go far deeper than that. Surely if people are forewarned of the risks, they can make better informed decisions? And by being explicit about the consequences, would it not potentially save

1 www.fca.org.uk/news/speeches/teamwork-smart-way-tackle-financial-crime

DOI: 10.4324/9781003588542-5

the banks vast sums of money on fraud prevention? Button, Shepherd, and Blackbourn recommended in 2016 that organisations should state clearly that fraudulent misrepresentations will lead to them being marked on a database for six years and that warnings should be more explicit in application forms.

I have had many discussions about the need for greater transparency with serving police officers and counter fraud professionals. The police and previous Conservative government agree that education is a vital component in the prevention of fraud. By educating people, they can then make informed decisions, potentially reducing the number of criminals and the supply of money mules for organised crime networks. Education will also help to protect the victims of fraud from ending up with fraud markers.

Monzo, Revolut, Starling, and other 'challenger' banks are attractive to young people because of their ease of use. However, all are behind the curve when it comes to fraud prevention measures because they cannot afford to invest the vast sums in counter-fraud technology and manpower as the main High Street banks. They have tended to have simple terms of business, rightly thinking that the last thing people want to read are pages of legal jargon. However, Monzo's terms and conditions have become more prescriptive over time, and the conclusion I draw from that is that Monzo has had to tighten up. The banks clearly recognise that there is a problem; they were told there was in the House of Lords Breaking the Chain report. Many have been making changes to their on-boarding processes for first-time account holders, directing them to apps and videos containing fraud awareness content. I hope that these initiatives will make a difference.

The AML systems are supposed to spot red flags and notify the relevant authorities when they see them and in the same process prevent potential customers from obtaining accounts or credit facilities. Obviously, those customers will try their luck elsewhere if they can, only to find that in the UK that they have been marked and so most organisations will not touch them. It is this light-touch, 'reasonable suspicion' approach which is formed out of AI, automated processes, and assumptions that has caused so many problems for so many, even if they are genuinely innocent of wrongdoing. It is a deliberately over-sensitive system. Reconciling the need for transparency against 'tipping off' provisions is going to require a delicate political juggling act. Legislation, such as the proposed Online Safety Bill, needs to be finalised and should emphasise more about fraud prevention and work with social media giants such as Meta to disrupt fraudulent content.

Is it right for private organisations to have unfettered 'state powers' over civilians, which sometimes exceed Article 8 ECHR principles?

To answer this question, there are three complicated but related issues that need to be considered. The first is to understand how Article 8 ECHR operates;

the second requires us to explore more about the threats that everyone is experiencing through the rise in deepfake and AI; and the last relates to some recent legislation.

The European Convention of Human Rights (ECHR) was established at the end of World War II and was ratified by the UK in 1951, which was the first nation to do so. Article 8 is of particular importance to those with bank accounts because it deals with data privacy. It states:

1. Everyone has the right to respect for his private and family life, his home and his correspondence.
2. There shall be no interference by a public authority with the exercise of this right except such as is in accordance with the law and is necessary in a democratic society in the interests of national security, public safety or the economic well-being of the country, for the prevention of disorder or crime, for the protection of health or morals, or for the protection of the rights and freedoms of others.[2]

Data should not be retained for longer than is necessary; the ICO's guidance to financial organisations states that data should not be retained for more than six years. I have seen several cases where data Subjects' details are not removed from databases automatically after six years; those are straightforward cases to rectify because the databases will voluntarily delete the data if requested to do so. In these instances, organisations have exceeded Article 8 ECHR principles.

Fraud marker appeal cases are not solely about data protection and privacy which result in damage to reputations. The FOS does not concern itself with Data Protection Act arguments or Article 8 (privacy) ECHR arguments on appeals against the imposition of fraud markers. Neither Cifas nor the FOS will consider Article 6 (fair trial and equality of arms) arguments. As a joint data controller, the fraud databases do have a duty to consider Article 8 arguments but sidestep the issues to the consideration of data retention only, leaving it for the member organisations that loaded the markers to justify their decisions to load and maintain markers. Cifas is the only database that will review the procedures followed. The FOS is only concerned with considering whether the organisation that loaded the marker acted 'reasonably' which, as explained earlier, provides a wider discretion than the courts. I have seen some decisions made by the FOS refer to whether organisations have acted 'fairly' or whether the outcomes of their decisions are 'fair'. Such comments imply that it might not be fair on the organisation to have to remove the marker in question. Surely fairness in this context means was it fair for a commercial agent of the state to protect the state and, by implication, the public interest? The issues

2 www.fra.europa.eu/en/law-reference/european-convention-human-rights-article-8-0

considered when markers are loaded relate to criminal law, imposing a reverse burden of proof on the data Subject to prove their innocence, and most appeal cases look no further than that.

Recently I was contacted by a solicitor who is a lecturer in law and an aspiring magistrate. During lockdown his wealthy elderly mother sent him £5,000 via an unauthorised money transfer agent in her home country. Santander spotted the transaction and questioned the source of funds; he explained he had no idea his mother was going to send him the money and did not know the sender of the funds. His account was closed. He became ill with Covid-related symptoms; when he eventually recovered he considered taking out a savings policy but his application was rejected, and the marker came to light. Before he could lodge a complaint to remove the marker his mother was taken ill and then sadly passed away. He has been debanked and marked. Should people in his position become collateral damage, sacrificed to the 'public interest' when they cannot prove their innocence? Should Santander use its discretion and remove this marker?

The European Court of Human Rights (ECtHR) has ruled:

> regard must be had in particular to the fair balance that has to be struck between the competing interests of the individual and of the community as whole, Subject in any event to the margin of appreciation enjoyed by the State.

The Court reiterated that 'the concept of private life extends to aspects relating to personal identity, such as a persons' name or physical and moral integrity, as well as to reputation and honour'.[3] The problem is that many people cannot prove their innocence which is a huge concern with incidents of data theft, malware, and deepfake rising. I question whether automated lending decision making processes are now fit for purpose. Deloitte predicts generative AI will cause losses to fraud of $40 billion in the US by 2027.[4] Can you imagine the impact if every victim of data theft was marked as a fraudster? Perfectly innocent, economically viable, decent, hardworking citizens whose lives would be in turmoil. If you think that is fantasy, think again. It is already happening.

In 2024 an interesting example of an innocent victim of identity fraud was reported by Shari Vahl on BBC's 'You and Yours' radio programme.[5] Chris, a retired head teacher who had lived at the same address for 32 years, received letters from Companies House confirming that his address had been registered as the correspondence address for a 'Mr Khan' and his company. Chris

3 Para 38 *Vincent Del Campo v Spain ECHT application number 25527/13*

4 www2.deloitte.com/us/en/insights/industry/financial-services/financial-services-industry-predictions/2024/deepfake-banking-fraud-risk-on-the-rise.html

5 Listen here www.bbc.co.uk/sounds/play/m001lrf6

commenced the lengthy process of getting Mr Khan removed from Companies House. In the meantime, he found himself marked by Sky with what sounded like a Cifas marker after Sky had refused to deliver a mobile phone he had ordered on the basis that it believed that a fraudster had applied for the new phone, not Chris. It transpired that several of Chris' neighbours had also been registered with Companies House in similar circumstances. To get himself removed as a Person of Significant Control of the fake company required a court order which cost Chris £300. The BBC reported that of 750,000 new companies registered with Companies House in 2022, 150,000 were fraudulent. As Chris put it when he was interviewed for the programme, it 'offends natural justice' that innocent people are marked and penalised in this way.

In August 2024, Cifas reported that 214,882 cases had been reported to the National Fraud Database between January and June 2024, 'an increase of 15% compared to the same period in 2023'.[6] It put much of the increase down to a 99% surge in facility takeovers and the practice of 'credit stuffing', 'the targeting of high volumes of accounts simultaneously, using multiple victims' personal information'. Many of those markers relating to facility takeovers will have been victims of impersonation markers, but I have a dreadful feeling that many innocent people will have been marked and debanked incorrectly.

I mentioned earlier that there is no such thing as a fair trial when it comes to appealing against Cifas markers. The reason is as follows. A fair trial is defined by Article 6(1) of the ECHR.[7] That convention is concerned with criminal proceedings rather than civil, establishing that 'everyone is entitled to a fair and public hearing within a reasonable time by an independent and impartial tribunal established by law'. Other than the FOS, the tribunals are not established by law and therefore do not need to be independent or impartial. It is for this reason that Article 8 arguments, respect for private life, rather than Article 6 rights to a fair trial and equality of arms, are applicable when considering fraud markers if the Subject can prove that they are innocent of wrongdoing or that the organisations have made mistakes. The fraud databases and member organisations rely on the argument that interference in private life can be justified in the interests of national security or for the prevention of crime, if it is necessary, proportionate and 'in accordance with the law'.[8]

Cifas's arbitration system can hardly be considered to comply with Articles 6 or 8. As joint data controller, is that right, and does that provide a proper arbitration procedure or access to fair justice?

Returning to Paul Marshall's article referred to in Chapter 3, he also discussed the failure of the Post Office to disclose evidence that might assist the defence. In civil cases, each party should disclose the evidence they wish to rely on to each other. In criminal cases the onus is on the prosecution to disclose all evidence,

6 www.fraudscape.co.uk

7 www.fra.europa.eu/en/law-reference/european-convention-human-rights-article-6

8 See *Malone v the United Kingdom – 8691/79 [1984] ECHR 10* (2 August 1984) (bailii.org)

including evidence that assists the defendant, which is fundamental to ensure a fair trial. But Marshall also pointed out that the only way the defendants in the Post Office Horizon prosecutions could prove their innocence was to be given access to the Post Office's internal records. There is therefore a parallel with organisations placing reliance on Data Protection Act exemptions[9] to withhold information that would assist a data Subject to successfully argue that a fraud marker should be removed. Thankfully many financial organisations do not adhere to those exemptions, but several do. Marshall's comments about the Post Office prosecutions will resonate with the innocent recipients of fraud markers; those who could defend themselves cannot unless they have access to the information held against them. If investigations were conducted thoroughly then many markers would not be loaded. Given the public's increased awareness of the impact of injustice following the Post Office Horizon scandal, organisations risk reputational damage if they continue to refuse to disclose information to assist a data Subject who may be innocent to help them prove their innocence. Where is the fair balance in refusing to co-operate with such requests? Are organisations being overly legalistic? The law is not perfect; many see the law as an ass[10] and struggle to access justice at the best of times.[11] Anyone with a fraud marker should take legal advice before asking the organisation that loaded it to remove it because a Final Response letter could have adverse long-term consequences for any subsequent appeal.

Finally, the legislative minefield concerns the Fail to Prevent Fraud offences created by sections 196 and 199 of the Economic Crime and Corporate Transparency Act 2023[12] (ECCTA). Are there any concerns about its potential application when considering whether to remove fraud markers?

Section 196 states:

> If a senior manager of a body corporate or partnership (the organisation) acting within the actual or apparent scope of their authority commits a relevant offence after this section comes into force, the organisation is also guilty of the offence.

That section is designed to enable prosecutors to look away from the controlling minds of companies; the legislation enables the prosecution of large organisations[13] for the actions of their employees.

9 www.ico.org.uk/for-organisations/uk-gdpr-guidance-and-resources/exemptions/a-guide-to-the-data-protection-exemptions

10 www.phrases.org.uk/meanings/the-law-is-an-ass.html

11 ww.lawsociety.org.uk/contact-or-visit-us/press-office/press-releases/only-one-in-five-believes-they-can-access-justice

12 For commentary see assets.publishing.service.gov.uk/media/65df57cfcf7eb1e5f4f57fdf/01.+ECCT+Bill+Overarching+Fact+Sheet.pdf

13 Defined by s202 ECCTA as having an aggregate turnover of more than £36 million net (or £43.2 million gross) and an aggregate balance sheet of more than £18 million net (or £21.6 million gross) and having more than 250 employees.

The organisations that are members of the databases are invariably large organisations and so are likely to fall under the remit of ECCTA. Have they perceived a risk that employees may aid and abet or procure within new customer on-boarding processes? The organisations benefit financially from opening accounts, so are they reasoning that, if they allow employees to move away from strict automated decision-making processes to on-board and then allow staff the discretion to remove fraud markers, then they risk prosecution if fraud is subsequently committed? Whilst an organisation would not necessarily be the victim, if it onboarded a fraudulent client then it could theoretically be accused of failing to prevent fraudulent activity; that could be the case if the on-boarding processes were less than rigorous or where an employee used their discretion to override automated processes or decided to remove a fraud marker. However, the legislation did not go as far as expected, and an offence is only committed by large organisations if a person who is associated with it commits a fraud offence intending to benefit their employer. There are statutory defences available under section 199(3) – where the body was the intended victim of the fraud offence – and under s199(4) if it had in place reasonable prevention procedures. Fraud offences are defined in Schedule 13 of the Act and include Theft Act 1968 (false accounting) and Fraud Act 2006 offences, but they do not include money laundering. Interestingly this legislation does appear to allow for large organisations to be marked to fraud databases in certain limited situations.

Although the ECCTA has strengthened anti-money laundering powers by providing additional powers to the NCA and has made it easier for businesses to share information with the police, I cannot see how it should hinder the removal of fraud markers against individual data Subjects. The banks and their employees would be overthinking the potential risk of prosecution for ECCTA offences were they to impose internal policies preventing the removal of markers; such policies would be unreasonable and contrary to the rules set out by Cifas and the other fraud databases, as well as exceeding Article 8 ECHR. In any event, the banks have a discretion not to readmit a customer, even if a fraud marker has been removed.

Is it right for the standard of proof for loading markers to be below that of criminal standard?

There are two sides to this argument. As previously discussed on one hand it can be argued that the plethora of suspicious banking transactions make it impossible for the banks to operate in any other way than to a civil, reasonable suspicion level. But, as the following examples demonstrate, huge injustice is caused to provably innocent recipients of fraud markers when organisations operate investigative systems that fall below the criminal standard. This is particularly so in relation to data theft and victims of impersonation cases, commonly found in application frauds and account takeover cases.

Cifas allows for the imposition of Victim of Impersonation markers (category 2). But, to load such markers organisations need to be convinced that the Subject in question is the victim of data or identity theft. With the rise of deepfake and generative AI, victims are much more difficult to spot. The banks are clearly taking the threat seriously, investing heavily in technology, systems, and learning, but it is obvious that genuine victims are more likely to be marked adversely. In such instances, organisations need to be open to thoroughly investigating the concerns raised and to be broad-minded about the level and nature of evidence provided to them. This criticism applies to the regulator too; the FOS must appreciate that the systems operated by criminals are likely to be more advanced than the technology used by the member organisations of the databases. The burden placed on the Subject challenging a marker must be lowered in such cases. If there is coherent evidence suggestive of innocence, then the benefit of the doubt should be provided.

The Post Office placed an over reliance on flawed technology[14] that had been given credibility by the law which stated that computer records must be presumed to be accurate unless shown to be otherwise. We know that criminals are far ahead of law enforcement and the banks in the technology that they use to commit crime. What the banks and law enforcement think is cutting edge and up to date might in fact be far behind the curve. Are the systems organisations use capable of detecting the most advanced frauds? Some organisations are far more advanced in their capabilities than others, and they can cause miscarriage of justice when their technology is flawed or out of date; they are not being held to account on this issue. If one organisation is able to spot deepfake or regenerative AI but another is not, then why should the advanced capabilities and intelligence of the more sophisticated bank be overruled in favour of the less advanced bank, as recently happened in a case where a challenger bank's marker was upheld against a Subject?

An example of flawed systems involved HSBC. Several clients came to me reporting a similar problem. All were purchasing buy-to-let properties through newly formed companies, but when the COVID-19 lockdown occurred, all had lost confidence in the property market and had decided to withdraw from the purchases. It transpired that all the clients had been sent funds back to their own new business accounts rather than solicitors' client accounts. For some reason HSBC had decided to load those applicants' details to Cifas. It appeared that the machine learning systems HSBC used had highlighted the transfers because they looked similar, and the systems saw these transactions as classic money laundering patterns. The first clients knew about it was when their other bank accounts started shutting down, causing them immense difficulties. I was able to argue successfully in each case that HSBC had made errors, which thankfully it admitted; it commendably agreed to pay all the clients' legal costs and some compensation.

14 For further reading see: journals.sas.ac.uk/deeslr/article/view/5172

Lack of understanding of the rules and inconsistency between organisations in their decision making is another area of concern. In this example, the owner of a business employing several members of staff found himself marked when, after his wife had transferred money to him to cover her tax bill, a few days later he was asked by her to return half of that money because she had lent it to someone. My client was concerned, and so he politely declined, reminding her that the money was required to pay her taxes. In response, his wife applied to her bank for a return of the funds she had requested. The culprit in this case was not her bank, which was blameless and acted correctly throughout. It had noticed that the funds had been paid from his wife's bank account and rightly informed his bank that it was going to investigate and that the funds should be held on account. However, my client's bank took this to mean that her bank had been informed of a fraud, and without asking any questions it immediately froze my client's account, closed it, terminated a loan account, and repaid itself from the funds my client put aside to pay his and his wife's tax bills. Then, to add insult to injury, it loaded a Cifas marker against my client. My client, obviously concerned, spoke to his wife's bank which confirmed that it had not even commenced an investigation. He was told it could not get involved with the Cifas marker loaded by his bank and that he should instruct a lawyer. The first of his bank's many errors were that no fraud had been identified, as confirmed by his wife's bank. His wife had directed her bank to transfer her money to her husband's account using two factor authentication. The transfer had been entirely consensual. Her bank had potentially ruined a successful business, wrecking more than 20 years hard work, causing him very difficult issues with his customers. Thankfully, the marker was removed.

I have many more examples of cases where the banks have admitted mistakes in their systems or have been forced to remove markers through arbitration. It is evident that there are instances of false positives in the investigation and reporting of markers, as reported by Dr Konstantinos Mersinas, Kathryn Westmore and Dr Alice Hutchings to the House of Lords' Fraud Act 2006 Digital Fraud Committee in a fascinating exchange with Viscount Colville of Culross.[15]

Another area of concern relates to the automated processes used in mortgage applications. Some lenders, like Yorkshire Building Society, insist on applications being made through mortgage brokers. However, such applications are not without risk. For example, I have had several cases where clients have been deceived by fraudulent mortgage brokers. I frequently see clients accuse brokers of submitting forged documents with applications without their knowledge. Proving that they are innocent or that the lenders have made mistakes is extremely difficult in such circumstances because the reporting systems require the organisations to load a marker on mere suspicion. Perhaps a return to the days of physically signed documentation would alleviate this problem?

15 See Q63 committees.parliament.uk/oralevidence/10018/pdf

It has become apparent that some organisations are more open than others in offering leniency to clients. As an example, a Subject came to me to help with an appeal he had already lodged. He had evidence that proved that the mortgage broker in question had been fraudulent and had been sacked by her employers when they realised that my client was not the only victim, and the broker in question had been struck off by their regulator. Despite that overwhelming evidence of innocence, in this case a Court was persuaded not to remove the marker by the lender that had loaded it. The argument the building society in question put forward was that it had done nothing wrong in loading the marker because it was a matter of fact that forged documents were submitted with the application and that Cifas had upheld its decision. It persuaded a district judge that, because Cifas had agreed with its reasoning, the Subject's application should be struck out. The result was a £15,000 costs award against the Subject and a CCJ that would add nearly six years of debanking to his pain. The Subject was rightly annoyed about the outcome and appealed. He was denied a fair trial based on a flawed system of arbitration that upheld a flawed decision. Had the client been charged with fraud he would have been exonerated; he had a strong defence to put forward, and it is doubtful whether the case would have passed the threshold test for the Code for Crown Prosecutors. The court agreed that the case should not have been struck out, and the organisation in question eventually withdrew its defence to the costs hearing on the basis that the marker was by then expired having run for the full six years.

The FOS repeatedly states in its decisions that fraud markers should not prevent someone from being able to access banking or credit facilities because organisations should consider each application individually. In practice I have seen fraud markers being used to provide financial organisations with the excuse to decline applications and to close accounts without explanation or question. Fraud markers have become a blanket use tool. For example, a property developer was marked by her lender on Cifas because there was a discrepancy with her employment history which it transpired had been incorrectly entered by her then mortgage broker when she applied for a personal mortgage. I managed to unravel that issue and have the Cifas marker removed. However, the marker had come to light because of a commercial mortgage application for her business. Despite being transparent with the commercial lender about the issue, sharing progress reports on the challenge, the commercial lender took the decision to withdraw its offer and load a marker against her with Synectics Solutions SIRA even though she had demonstrated her innocence all along. The Synectics Solutions marker was removed in due course but not without causing added and unnecessary stress, cost, and undue complications, a demonstration that one financial organisation will interpret rules and 'contractual obligations' differently to others.

In the most extreme example of the cruelty that can experienced when banks incorrectly refuse to remove fraud markers, a final response letter from NatWest read simply: 'I am advised that we are unable to remove the marker'. In this case it was an inappropriate and unsympathetic response; my client was the victim of the most horrendous domestic abuse, as the bank was fully aware. Her story covers many of the issues discussed elsewhere in this book. It is a tragic tale. I have anonymised her details, but she was keen for me to share her story. She had met her husband when he worked for a bank, and she required funding for her successful business. He soon showered her with attention and, believing herself to be in love, they married. However, it transpired that her husband was in fact a fraudster who had to resign from the bank he was working for when an investigation was commenced into suspicious activities. He joined another FCA regulated business but again got himself into hot water and resigned just after another investigation commenced. Forced to go his own way, he turned his attention on my client's family, persuading her retired mother to invest in a rental property portfolio. But the property portfolio was never built, and the money was never repaid, forcing her mother to sell her home and move in with my client's sister. My client had the foresight to ensure that all mail sent to her mother's former home was redirected, and it became apparent over time that her husband was setting up fake companies to that address as well as taking out loans and falsifying identification documents. In the meantime, my client was Subjected to extreme physical violence resulting in injury, and she was forced to apply for a Non-Molestation Order. Not being a wealthy woman, although her business gave her a comfortable level of income, and without her own home (she lived in a rented flat because her husband always claimed he could not afford to purchase a home, even though he spent plenty of money frequently changing his cars), she could not afford to commence divorce proceedings given the Non-Molestation Order had cost her a five figure sum. Then, to her horror, she discovered that she had had a Cifas marker loaded against her by a finance company she had used previously; the marker was for 'false application fraud'. Her husband had attempted to deceive one of NatWest's subsidiaries into loaning him £70,000 supporting his application with fake documents which used her address. Her husband was sophisticated and clever with experience of working in the banking and finance industry and he had had every opportunity to steal her identity. The file we put together to the finance company was the most comprehensive I have ever assembled. There were several hundreds of pages of documents, all pointing to her fraudster husband as being responsible. Infuriatingly, and unfathomably, justice was denied; NatWest refused to remove the marker. She had by then been given notice on her flat and her business premises and because many landlords and tenant referencing agencies now use the Cifas database, she was unable to find a new home for herself or her business. But by then NatWest had placed her Bounce Back Loan into default. She did not have the funds or the stomach to continue her fight for justice. Since she was claiming that she was not the customer, the FOS would not have considered her appeal. Cifas would have been her only arbiter. Her mental health declined and following a desperate call from her in which I was left in no doubt that she was about to attempt suicide I called the police who thankfully went to her immediate assistance. She did not have the stomach to take her appeal further.

Other organisations have been prepared to be more lenient and remove fraud markers when Subjects can prove their innocence. Take for example the company director who relied on his secretary to submit some documents to a car insurance company, only for her to send the wrong one. Then the young entrepreneur who closed one account and moved funds to another account, only for the sending bank to incorrectly send an alert. Or the lady who applied for finance to have teeth repaired, only for it to be rejected incorrectly. The bank employee who was alleged to have falsified a CV; it transpired that he had not made false claims, as had been alleged. The accountant who unwittingly acted for a fraudster. I have many other examples. But there is so much inconsistency in decision making that some of the cases mentioned earlier would have gone the other way had they had facilities with other organisations.

Many of those cases would not have come to my attention had a criminal standard of proof been applied and thorough investigations taken place. Commercial expedience and cost control is no excuse for organisations to reduce standards, especially when injustice can be caused. If organisations wish to provide services to the public, then they should ensure they can dedicate sufficient resource to protect their customers. If they cannot afford to do that, then it is arguable that they should not be allowed a licence to trade. If that reduces choice and increases costs to the consumer, then is that a price worth paying to ensure that the risk of injustice through debanking is reduced?

Conclusion

According to the Cambridge Dictionary, justice means 'fairness in the way people are dealt with' or, in a legal context, 'the system of laws in a country that judges and punishes people'.[16] Having read this book, one may reach the conclusion that the fraud marker system and its associated appeal mechanisms have nothing to do with fairness at all.

One of the most vocal critics of the fraud marker system is Professor Ian Ross who told me:

> There are three main issues affecting banks and their approach to fraud. First is an institutional culture across banking of working in silos. When it comes to fraud this is a seismic fault. A customer who calls reporting being scammed speaks to a customer service operative first (an operative who doesn. . .'t know what fraud is) who decides if it will go to the "fraud department" but via management. By the time the report reaches the fraud department locked away in an office somewhere, the account is nothing like it was when the customer reported it. The complaint is watered down and reshaped into a narrative that suits policy and not the customer.

16 dictionary.cambridge.org/dictionary/english/justice

> Inevitably in the vast majority of cases nothing gets done about it often. Also, one global bank was discovered to be "fiddling figures" by diverting complaints into a "customer feedback gateway" to keep complaints figures down and said bank can get "customer service" of the year award. Fraud departments meanwhile act like some elitist unit. This tracks inevitably to their training. Over my 20 years of professional training delivery including with banks globally, the highest level of training staff receive is a supervised "AML" e-learning course. As for investigators this is a misnomer, given that they rarely investigate. The rejectionist customer-blaming attitudes to victims of fraud, their customers are entrenched institutionally. Experience shows that when a customer complains of being scammed via their accounts or such as "advanced payment fraud" the risk people look for loopholes in the wording of the complaint. In short, that means that the banks only "investigate" an issue when it affects the bank: either financially, or reputationally. Not a finger is stirred to support a customer who has been fleeced thorough their account. Shown by the total absence of court convictions and token appearances in bank groups with once-a-year meetings, and email-shotting to customers about fraud awareness. So-called dedicated card fraud police units merely exist to maintain profits. A massive irony of course is that this customer-blaming goes full circle when a bank operative receives a report from CIFAS about a "suspicious" customer. The allegations are glorified smear with no evidence of fraud. But the customer suddenly finds her or himself labelled as a fraudster with no legal basis. Effectively branded by use of these asinine fraud markers, the knock-on effects of which can be catastrophically life-changing for the customer. Being de-banked without cause, accounts frozen, being rendered unemployable through no fault of their own. The culture and attitudes go full circle.

I am personally uncomfortable with the fact that many of the investigators employed by banks are untrained. I know many counter-fraud professionals working in the banking and finance communities who are highly qualified, certified to professional standards, and are enthusiastic and dedicated to their work. Counter-fraud provides good, stimulating, and rewarding career opportunities. I want to understand more about why there is an apparent disconnect between the professionals I know and respect and their siloed unqualified colleagues.

The concept of fair banking is more concerned with ensuring that the products and services offered by financial organisations are fair.[17] As demonstrated, fraud markers are loaded and policed by private organisations, with some organisations paying little regard to common notions of justice and fairness. Their decisions can be unfair, cruel even. I am concerned at the level of injustice I see, every day. Lack of space has not permitted to me to provide

17 www.fca.org.uk/firms/fair-treatment-customers

more examples, but that concern was the driver for me to write this book. People are being genuinely wronged. Granted, fraud markers do an important job, but the collateral damage I have witnessed makes me question whether the systems are fit for purpose in some instances, and I am concerned about the potential negative economic impact fraud markers could cause in the future. Criminals are setting up fake businesses using real identities to obtain banking and finance facilities; the debanked innocent victims of such practices are at real risk of never finding justice.

In September 2024 the FCA published its 'UK payment accounts access and closure: update' report.[18] The FCA expressed concern that the banks showed an inconsistency of approach in how they record data and found evidence of the inaccurate recording of data. Some files were not retained or contained limited information on the reason for closures. It criticised lack of consistency with firms regarding how reputational risk was managed, and firms lacked clear data regarding the reasoning, resulting in firms potentially not acting 'in good faith'. The report reminded firms of their duties under the Consumer Duty which was fully effective from 31 July 2024 to keep good records of its reasoning for refusing to onboard or offboard a customer on the grounds of reputational risk. The report caveated that the data it reviewed pre-dated the Consumer Duty coming into force. The Consumer Duty moves towards outcome focussed principals like those found in other professions such as law and accountancy. It is hoped that this duty, which includes more emphasis on regulated firms acting fairly, will result in a more positive approach to assessing whether to debank and load fraud markers.

Businesses are being debanked at an alarming rate and do not have the regulatory protection provided to retail customers. Tucked away towards the end of the FCA's September report was the recognition that non-retail customers (i.e. anything other than micro-enterprise business) and charities are not being supported by the current regulatory framework. The report mentioned that in France and Belgium there is a legal right, a 'universal service obligation', that could be replicated in the UK, but that would be a matter for Parliament and government.

The dilemma is that fraud markers are important and have undoubtably disrupted a vast amount of criminal activity. The majority of the two million plus Cifas markers that are in existence are probably justifiable. However, a fairer balance must be struck to protect those who genuinely protest – and can prove – their innocence. If Cifas is upholding 16.6% of complaints based purely on procedural failings, then if one extrapolates that figure it is possible that at least several hundred thousand current markers have been incorrectly loaded and are 'unfair'. Organisations must accept that, when Subjects

18 See www.fca.org.uk/publications/corporate-documents/uk-payment-accounts-access-and-closures-update

challenge markers, perfection of evidence is not always possible. In my opinion a reverse burden placed on the Subject based on the balance of probabilities would be justified and desirable, particularly in data theft and identity takeover cases.

There has never been a greater threat from organised crime networks. The banks are getting better at spotting financial crime and are on a seemingly never-ending escalator of learning, helped by the likes of Alexander Wood, who I mentioned earlier and who wrote the forward to this book. He is a reformed hyper-prolific offender who was responsible for many of the highest profile financial crimes in recent years. Other than impersonating the thirteenth Duke of Marlborough to defraud many five-star hotels in London, he committed multi-million pounds worth of cyber-crime.[19] He has now become a keynote speaker and advisor to government and the banking industry to help them better understand the 'fraud mindset', sophisticated social engineering techniques, and the threat of emerging technology including the increased use by criminals of artificial intelligence. His work is enabling a better understanding of the use and operation of mule accounts used to launder the proceeds of criminal activity. Hopefully that work will mean more effective targeted use of debanking and fewer innocent account holders being incorrectly marked.

On 21 September 2023 a webinar was arranged for members of Cifas, Equifax, and National Hunter entitled *Are fraud data consortiums the future for fraud prevention?* It was interesting that Synectics Solutions was not advertised as being part of that panel. When I was researching this book, Professor Mark Button[20] kindly sent me a copy of the report he co-authored in 2016, which I have referred to previously. It concluded that the fraud databases should work together to harmonise standards. The report invited the creation of a code of practice bringing together consumers, regulators and counter-fraud professionals, which if not voluntary then might need to be regulated. The report talked about reform to ensure that decisions were fair for everyone and based on a high standard of investigation. It was prophetic thinking and should be revisited, and I would like to see an update on the meeting that took place between Cifas, Equifax, and National Hunter. As with the failure of the banks to learn lessons from HBOS, lessons are not being learned quickly enough by the counter-fraud, banking, and finance communities to supress the growing public concern of the perceived abuse of power by organisations. It is, however, heartening that some of the databases are open to leading that discussion, and it is hoped that their member organisations will engage positively. In the past couple of years, I have experienced a

19 See Live Talk: Combatting Fraud by Eliminating Mule Accounts (govnet.co.uk)

20 Director of the Centre for Cybercrime and Economic Crime at the School of Criminology and Criminal Justice, University of Portsmouth

willingness by some organisations to act with more consideration and fairness to those challenging fraud markers, notably Barclays, Lloyds, Nationwide, and Monzo; none are pushovers. Others, however, appear to have gone backwards, which is regrettable and concerning. I have also recently noticed that some banks are loading markers that last for three years rather than the usual six where young people have been suspected of money mule activity; I applaud that approach.

The debanking and Post Office Horizon scandals have clearly demonstrated two uncomfortable truths for the UK. It has now moved into a legal system where innocence must be proved; the presumption of innocence has been eroded. And through a combination of long-standing power-creep, negligence, incompetence, and a smattering of dishonesty it has also come dangerously close to being controlled by a system of corporate authoritarianism.

As explained previously, politicians from all parties are aware of the issues explored in this book; many of them have first-hand experience of being debanked. The banking and finance community need to remember that they are privileged to have the powers that have been bestowed on them, but if they cross the line of what is regarded as acceptable, fair, and just behaviour, then Parliament will reconsider whether those powers should be limited and Subjected to more rigorous regulatory intervention and penalties.

As demonstrated earlier, the systems used by Cifas, Synectics Solutions, and National Hunter work in different ways, albeit with some crossover, and I recognise that they can be extremely important tools in the fight against fraud and money laundering. But the Synectics Solutions and National Hunter systems are in particular open to abuse, and there is no concept of fairness or justice built into their decision-making processes; they allow for more automated lending decisions to be made but at some risk to consumers given the rapid ascent of deepfake and AI in identity takeover.

The advice I offer to nations looking to replicate the fraud marker system in the UK is that they should ensure that: fair, transparent arbitration systems are freely available to their citizens; financial organisations are placed under a duty to consider cases fairly, impartially, and transparently with clear guidance and discretion allowed; an Ombudsman system should not be defined by strict rules preventing access to a form of justice for significant groups within society; and fraud awareness education and training should be promoted and considered key in the fight against fraud and money laundering.

In the UK, even with some safeguards in place, the nightmare for many innocent Subjects has already moved from dystopian into reality.

Index

FSC
www.fsc.org
MIX
Papier | Fördert
gute Waldnutzung
FSC® C083411

Kolibri 360 GmbH
Ferdinand-Jühlke-Straße 7
99095 Erfurt, Deutschland
produktsicherheit@kolibri360.de